Cupcakes, Yoga and Jesus

Overcoming the sticky situation of Addiction

Dr. Lyn G. Litchke

WESTBOW
PRESS®
A DIVISION OF THOMAS NELSON
& ZONDERVAN

Cover design by Ann Gorbett
Interior art by Dr. Lyn (aka Lil Luna)
Photos of Author by Charlotte Cavanaugh

Scripture quotations are taken from the Holy Bible, New Living Translation, copyright ©1996, 2004, 2007, 2013, 2015 by Tyndale House Foundation. Used by permission of Tyndale House Publishers, Inc., Carol Stream, Illinois 60188. All rights reserved. Scripture quotes marked (NKJV) are taken from the New King James Version®. Copyright © 1982 by Thomas Nelson. Used by permission. All rights reserved.

WestBow Press books may be ordered through booksellers or by contacting:

WestBow Press
A Division of Thomas Nelson & Zondervan
1663 Liberty Drive
Bloomington, IN 47403
www.westbowpress.com
1 (866) 928-1240

Because of the dynamic nature of the Internet, any web addresses or links contained in this book may have changed since publication and may no longer be valid. The views expressed in this work are solely those of the author and do not necessarily reflect the views of the publisher, and the publisher hereby disclaims any responsibility for them.

Any people depicted in stock imagery provided by Thinkstock are models, and such images are being used for illustrative purposes only. Certain stock imagery © Thinkstock.

ISBN: 978-1-5127-6905-0 (sc)
ISBN: 978-1-5127-6907-4 (hc)
ISBN: 978-1-5127-6906-7 (e)

Library of Congress Control Number: 2016921040

Print information available on the last page.

WestBow Press rev. date: 2/7/2017

*To my husband, Scott, my two sons, Nic and Zac,
my stepchildren, Sammy and Jared.*

And to my daddy and sweet sisters, Gina and Nina.

CONTENTS

FOREWORD

by Zac Saunders

My mom invited me to write this foreword so you would understand my side of the story. Our hope is that this book will help another family avoid the numerous landmines we stepped on trying to navigate the tricky terrain of addiction. I trust when you read our story you will find some peace and know you are not alone. There is a power that comes from knowing you are not alone.

I suppose I should start where it all began. Growing up, I knew my parents loved me, but I just needed more attention. Everyone was so busy. I needed a more direct influence. My family spent less and less time together, getting more and more disconnected. My parents worked more and more. My dad ran his own business. My mom was in school and working. They were all stressed out. I think they convinced themselves that if they worked more out of love and financial survival, those were justifiable reasons. But what they didn't address was that they were spending less and less time with me. There is a vicious cycle where parents get so stressed they get divorced. Mine did. The way my mom coped was through drinking wine. It was what she knew to do. All those times, I would get so upset in my room. If I had just had something to do with my body and my feelings, I could have dealt with it better. Yoga sure would have helped back then.

Being disconnected from a busy family can lead to the inability to successfully and healthily connect with other people. How are you supposed to connect with others when you can't even connect with your family? Following disconnection can be this out-of-control selfishness. Addicts are selfish. Seeking connection to drugs is a selfish act. We want to feel comforted. Drugs may do the job temporarily, but ultimately they leave you feeling isolated and closed off. Drugs do not discriminate between those who are privileged and those who are underprivileged. Drugs don't care if you're rich or poor or have a GED or a PhD. If all the circumstances, such as family history and stressful life events, align just right, you may become a victim to the allure of drugs and alcohol. It was certainly nothing new to our family. My mom participated in recreational drugs and alcohol from a young age. So it is no wonder that as a young boy coming of age, I came to know them too. I was trying to fill that void inside me. I needed something. But I wasn't sure what that something was. I developed a nasty habit that led to an addiction, just like my mom. I believe addiction affects 100 percent of the population, if not directly at least indirectly. Before I go any further, ask yourself this … do you or anyone you know have a problem with drugs or alcohol? It may be the most important question of your life. And the answer even more so.

Probably like most kids, I transitioned from needing my parents' attention to needing gratification from my peers at school. In eighth grade, I won the middle school counselors' award for being a good friend. I was the teacher's pet. I got straight As up till high school. That's when I met my two friends. They were cool and befriended me. I thought that maybe I might be cool and good-looking too. I could be the bad boy and get the girls. I began smoking weed way too young because of the pressure of wanting to be cool and fit in. In those moments of vulnerability, I just wanted to be loved and accepted. I wish I was cool enough to feel established in myself, to not feel the need for validation from others, but I wasn't. Instead, I was the nervous nelly of the group. *Maybe we shouldn't do this.* Later on, in trying to make sense of it all, I started doing cocaine. Being lost and being popular. That's when I really messed up my brain chemistry, probably almost permanently. My least proud thing to say about myself. Stealing money from my parents. Stealing my brother's car at night. Getting into others' cars and doing drugs. I remember being so paranoid about getting in trouble. Then I met my girlfriend, and we had way too much in common. That attraction led to some more poor decisions.

What's school got to do with it? Teachers have such a hard job with more than twenty kids in the class to parent. They are not to blame. There was this authoritarian aspect of our school system at the time where kids were forced by law to go to school or their parents got fined $5,000 or went to jail. (It has since been repealed.) How was that supposed to help me learn to help myself and understand what was happening to my body and mind? The teachers said, "We have to leave it to your parents to tell you about those issues." When did my parents have time for that? I did what I was told to do, unless I didn't understand. I remember in fifth grade, I did not like to tuck in my shirt, which was one of our rules that I did not understand. I asked a teacher why. The teacher replied, "It is easier for you to hide a gun in a waistband." I was nine. How do you say that to a nine-year-old? I was left with this strange confusion. It made me uncomfortable to tuck in my shirt. Really, that's the concern?

No wonder teen depression is through the roof. What is causing these issues? How I wish that yoga and mindfulness were taught in my health or physical education courses. Why is there only physical education and not psychological education? What about my psyche and my spirit? No stress management techniques whatsoever. All I could think back then in school was ... *Right here, right now, anybody just tell me how to get through the day*! Just having this whole giant day ahead of me was so overwhelming, and that was at the *beginning* of every day. Getting started was the hardest part. Having negative speech. What did so and so think of me? The mind is so susceptible to negative thoughts. The path of least resistance. The goal is being happy and not thinking negatively. Negativity is a shroud over positivity. Our true nature is covered up by thoughts of the mind. Positivity is like paddling upstream heading toward your *happy* destination, all the while knowing there's a giant waterfall behind you.

I remember feeling like the science information I was learning in school or researching online just seemed like atheism was becoming more and more prevalent. That somehow I was becoming less significant, with no control over my situation. I started to get the impression from Western thinkers, I am a fluke. I am insignificant, and everything is meaningless. There is nothing special about what is going on. What is the point of being alive if we are all going to die and the world is so harsh to live in? Those were the eyes I was looking through, with no way to understand that these arguments go both ways. I am just as significant as insignificant. The world is just as hard as it is beautiful. I would learn later that yoga helps us understand our place in the universe. The practice of yoga is maintenance of our consciousness. If you feel you are the universe, you are Gigantic! You are a part of everything! The vibe that I got from science in school was OMG the universe is so big and I am so small. But through the lens of yoga, compared to the size of an atom, we are just as big as we are small.

I had this thought ... what about instead of saying the Pledge of Allegiance every day in school, we could recite, "I am beautiful. I am loved. There's divinity inside me. The conscious awareness inside of me is in everything. Even though we appear different and separate, we are one." That is what yoga teaches. Some schools are not allowed to teach yoga due to a connection to Hinduism. Parents are concerned it is a religious form of mind-body exercise, not spirituality. Parents need to read "Beyond 'Namaste': The benefits of yoga in schools" (Santas 2016).

But what if yoga, mindfulness, and stress management were taught in school along with a more comprehensive education of drugs, based on facts, not law? Maybe there would not be so much misinformation. And way better coping skills. The very same people who told me not to do drugs were daily drinking coffee and taking medication for attention disorders or tiredness. Leaving me stumped. Are there good addictions? Or are they all bad addictions? Are there more acceptable and less acceptable addictions? What is the difference between drug use and abuse? Some people are prescribed meds for the rest of their lives, and some people decide to smoke a plant in the morning. Are there functional and dysfunctional addictions and behaviors? Even little things like coffee every morning manipulate the chemistry in your brain. Some people can't function or go to work without coffee. If you are an addict and you do it every single day, it is going to manifest itself in a bad way. After all, too much of a good thing is bad—right? Drugs in general are just plain hard to define.

The point I am trying to make is there are acceptable instances when people can choose to use drugs responsibility. There is a lot of confusion about plants as drugs. Many people who ingest plants have the most profound experience of their life, promoting feelings of connection to other people and those around them. Plants connect us to the earth and others. It's a magical feeling, yoga and plants. Plants do it more quickly and intensely and don't require the yoga practice aspect of *tapas* (discipline) of Niyamas. If meditation and yoga are the course to understanding the nature of consciousness, then plant medicine represents the crash course. Maybe it's because we are so disconnected from the world and each other, we just keep searching.

I did not find yoga till I was twenty-one and had hit rock bottom. I was going to jail. My mom introduced me to it to help me (and herself) cope with the enormity of the situation. However, by the time I was released from jail, I felt very, very static. I spent an incredible amount of time in bed. I did not feel like I should eat and drink when other kids were starving.

Why live in this place that is so evil? My analysis of this world left me paralyzed. I lived under a blanket of ignorance, seeing the world through eyes not open. Where had all this stuff come from? I needed compassion. I needed yoga. So while this world seemingly was separate and harsh, if I looked past the surface and devoted my attention inward, there was this whole other part of the world I discovered that was beyond physical. That you can't even touch or smell. You can only experience it in your heart. You remember the other side of the world and your connection to the miracle that life is. You are astonished and excited for whatever comes. You have faith. You are a part of something bigger than you.

I felt comforted that I was in control and out of control at the same time. Each day I did my best to remember the truth. The truth is that I am not my body. I am not the world. I am something that both constitutes and transcends the universe. God transcends the duality of life and death. I am the spirit. I believe in God and Jesus. I think He was meant to be believed in as not something totally tangible. He is metaphorical.

My understanding of God comes through yoga and other experiences I have had with medicinal plants. All these things we stress out about need to be dealt with. We need to turn and face these monstrous challenges that become our interpersonal and international issues. This is the strength we can cultivate together through mindfulness and understanding. Even though we are different, our individuality and self-expression should be celebrated; we are ultimately all equal. There is a whole other realm that goes beyond the drama of my everyday life. I try to remember that realm is in me.

In closing, this story represents a small reflection of a large issue that has many underlying factors. Take a second and look around, as unbiased as you can. There's something going on, and we are the proof. The universe is a conscious, living, growing thing because it produces conscious living and growing things. I would say if my life were a tree, I burst out of my seed and grew like a weed. But I did encounter a cloud that slowed my development. It took time for me to find the sunlight again and continue on with my development. The goal is seeing through the clouds of ignorance and negativity. Enlightening yourself to the true loving nature of your own soul. And letting that shine through the darkness of the unknown. After all, God pursues us in the dark. I believe the truth is that you have nothing to fear. All that there ever was, always will be changing, forever and ever, and we're just along for the ride. Allan Watts (2016) says it best: "We do not come into this world; we come out of it. Just as the apple comes out of the tree, we are the fruit of the world. 'Peopling' is what the world does. Making apples is what an apple tree does."

Hey, Mom,
Love you eternally,
Zac

PREFACE

The following story represents a mother's journey through addiction and salvation. Turning a midlife crisis into a midlife transformation. It is all said with *think* preparation: the *t*ime is right, now; *h*onestly, as best I can recall; *i*nspired, from my heart, *n*ecessary, to heal; and with *k*indest words possible.

Four years ago, I was an active alcoholic, and my son was behind bars for drugs. We found Jesus on both sides of those bars (or He found us). Today my son is tobacco- and cocaine-free. I am alcohol-free. I found joy in baking cupcakes instead of drinking wine. My cupcakes feature messages about Jesus, so I can spread His word one cupcake at time.

To celebrate my second year of sobriety, I began making bumper stickers to share how God turned my craving for wine into a craving for Him instead. My car is covered with them. People pull up behind me and point, read, laugh, smile, and even take pictures. I have become a mobile and delicious messenger for Jesus.

A certain author inspired me to take "Operation Love Does" and give it my personal spin. One of my college students, Meagan, gave me his book and said she saw some Bob in me. I had no idea, till I met him, what a huge compliment that was. Here's to "Living on the Edge of Yikes," Bob Goff! I have purchased at least a dozen of his books and given them away to those who are on a quest to explore Jesus.

For ten years of my son's life, I used to fear his phone calls because I knew he was in so much pain, and I was trying so desperately to save him. But one day he called and told me he gave a man at work CPR and saved his life. So if you are in need of a miracle today, keep on reading this book because miracles happen every day. My first twelve miracles are revealed in the following pages. So read on, and let the healing commence.

CHAPTER 1

COURAGE TO CHANGE

I have three birthdays. Not everyone can say that, but I can. I have my *Belly Button Birthday*, my *Born Again Birthday*, and my *Sober Birthday*. If you are in recovery or have become a Christian later in life, you probably have heard these terms. My Belly Button Birthday began on February 12, 1960 in Cleveland, Ohio. I was born into an Irish, Italian, Catholic family. I was the middle of three girls. Not surprising, as the middle child I grew up to be the black sheep. My dad traveled a lot, and my mom stayed home with us girls. My mom would be our disciplinarian all week, and then my dad would come home and burst through the door only to be mobbed by three giggling, screaming, excited daughters. He brought us gifts, laughter, and joy. I think my mom did the best that she could. But she had a habit that was befuddling to me as a child. She would seemingly out of the blue get really upset, start yelling and screaming, then run upstairs crying. I was left behind wondering, *What in the world just happened? What did I do wrong? What did I not do right? What should I do now to make her stop crying and come back? What can I do so she loves me? What if she doesn't come back?* In my little-girl mind, I heard a voice saying, "I promise I will be perfect, Mommy. Please come back." Hence my lifelong quest to try to figure out how to be "perfect."

My dad would always try to smooth things over and come upstairs later as I went to bed and tell me that she was just stressed out trying to do everything during the week without him there. My dad always used humor to ease my discomfort. He would get on top of my bed and say he felt bumps and lumps and couldn't get comfortable while pretending he didn't know I was under the covers. My tears turned to small giggles as he tried his best to reassure me and put my doubts to rest. But I never talked about it with my mom, ever. Sadly, she died of ovarian cancer when I was thirty-three (she was sixty), and my ultimate fear was realized. She was not coming back. I would never be able to make myself *perfect* enough.

Why is it you always remember things from your childhood that are tragic way more than you remember the good stuff? I seem to be able recall in vivid detail my most painful moments of life. For example, at the age of thirteen, during my seventh grade year at a Catholic school, I spent the night at a friend's house where her parents proceeded to introduce me to keg beer. I puked all night long and cried about how much I loved my friend, her siblings, and parents. The next morning, I was hungover for the first time. Little did I know that would be the first of many hangovers to follow. Needless to say, no one mentioned a word to me about it. I was returned home with the claim that I was sick. Message received: "Do not talk about it!"

Fast-forward to my four years at a public high school. I blossomed into a popular homecoming queen, gymnast, cheerleader, and—you guessed it—binge drinker. I drank most weekends. I shot a 3.2 beer before I cheered at every football game. I had no problem climbing to the top of the pyramid. I dated the quarterback of the football team. At the homecoming dance, I proceeded to get him banned from the homecoming game after sneaking my friend out to our car to drink the alcohol I had brought. I accidently (drunkenly) left the car door open, and the police found the booze. He did not speak to me for fifteen years.

I snuck alcohol from my house, with easy access to our liquor cabinet. My parents drank every night at five for happy hour. Dad would cook kielbasa on the grill, and we all shared this joyous time together as a family. How could alcohol be bad if the love and happiness I felt every day at five was so good? My parents were golfers and led active social lives. Alcohol just seemed to coincide with every event. I drove the refreshment (beer) golf cart for our country club. I was an avid swim team competitor too, all while binge drinking on weekends. I was a top student. I won tons of academic awards. Teachers loved me, and I them. I loved school and learning. This carried me as far as a PhD. I was a top master's female triathlete in my forties for eight years, drinking every day at five o'clock. That is all part of this mysterious disease of alcoholism. Very tricky that alcohol. In the *Big Book of Alcoholics Anonymous* (AA), it says, "Alcohol is cunning, baffling and powerful!" (Smith and Wilson 2001, 58–59). Well, I will attest to that. How could I be an alcoholic if I could graduate ninth in my high school class of two hundred, get numerous academic awards, and be homecoming queen? I had a 4.0 in my master's and doctoral program.

Now just wait one minute. Why is it you have to "detox" from alcohol? Doesn't the mere definition of detox mean to rid the body of toxic, unhealthy substances (Carr 2005)? Doesn't that mean alcohol is poison? Allen Carr goes on to describe in his book about the fly and the pitch plant. He clearly explained what was happening when I drank. I had become the fly. Go figure, a smart girl like me did not figure that out till the age of fifty-one. How is it possible I missed that message?

No surprise that my college years and adulthood were plagued with one bad decision after another—mostly under the influence of alcohol. I fell away from religion and practicing Catholicism. I became selfish, especially in relationships. I did not know how to be a part of a healthy relationship. I hightailed it out of two failed marriages that produced two sons I love dearly. I was busy trying to find the love that I did not feel from my mother. I was going to make sure my sons knew I loved them no matter what. And they do. They are the best two things I have done on this earth.

I look back now at the insecurity that I felt in my own home, with my own mother, and I realize that all I wanted was to feel love and security. Unfortunately, I had linked love strongly to alcohol. I was predestined to confuse alcohol and love for over thirty years. I went on to my third marriage with my drinking buddy and best friend. We have practiced controlled, high-functioning, alcoholic behavior for over twenty years together. Hmmm ... go figure that one.

As I approached my second birthday, I began to get the *courage to change*. With a cherry on top!

Courage to Change Chocolate-Covered Cherry Cappuccino Cupcake (C6)

(Makes 24 cupcakes)

Cupcake Ingredients:
2 cups cake flour
3/4 cup dark coco powder
1 1/2 teaspoon baking soda
1 pinch salt
1/2 teaspoon cinnamon
1 stick unsalted butter, softened
1 1/2 cups light brown sugar
2 large eggs, room temperature
1/2 cup sour cream, room temperature
3/4 cup freshly brewed coffee
2 tablespoons espresso powder

Filling:
1 (16-ounce) can cherry pie filling

Frosting:
1/2 cup heavy whipping cream
12 ounces cream cheese
1 teaspoon vanilla
1 pinch salt
1/2 cup powder sugar

Garnish and Topper:
24 chocolate-covered espresso beans or cherry candies
coco powder to dust top
24 coffee stirrer sticks
24 "Courage to Change" sayings
24 straw toppers
24 scrapbook pattern paper cutouts for coffee mug

Directions:

Cupcakes:
- Preheat oven to 350 degrees F. Line cupcake tins with brown or tan color-stay cupcake papers.
- Sift flour, coco powder, baking soda, salt, and cinnamon in separate bowl.
- In electric mixer, whip butter till smooth.
- Add brown sugar and eggs one at a time till fluffy.
- Add dry ingredients alternating with sour cream and mix just till incorporated.
- Whisk espresso powder into coffee. Add to batter just till combined.
- Fill cupcake liners half-full. Then follow filling directions below before baking.

Filling:
- Scoop cherry pie filling into a piping bag.
- Cut hole in bottom of bag large enough for cherries to be expelled.
- Squeeze into center of cupcake batter.
- Bake for 18–22 minutes till toothpick comes out clean. Cool completely.

Frosting:
- In electric mixer on high, whip heavy cream till it peaks. Scoop into small bowl. Set aside.
- In same mixer, beat cream cheese, vanilla, salt, and powder sugar on low speed till blended.
- Fold in whip cream just till blended.
- Put in piping bag and swirl on top of cooled cupcakes.

Garnish and Topper:
- Cut out small sayings. Use glue gun to adhere saying to straw toppers. Slide over coffee stirrer.
- Cut out coffee cup shape with handle from scrapbook pattern paper. Wrap around cupcake and glue on inside of handle.
- Garnish with espresso bean or cherry candy.
- Dust with cocoa powder.

CHAPTER 2

GO BANANAS FOR GOD!

I celebrated my *Born Again Birthday* with a phone call from my twenty-one-year-old son. It was his one phone call from jail. And no, I don't want you to talk about this! But I have to. I cannot hide from the truth anymore. My words may help another mother or son out there. Oh, and God told me to tell the world about Him. More on that later.

Before I received that phone call, I need to tell you how we got there. When my son was thirteen (what an unlucky number), my neighbor shared the delightful news with me that my son was passed out behind the shrubs in our yard the other night. She said to me, "I thought you should know." This was the first of many signs that I would choose to ignore. Denial at its finest. I dealt with the situation the best way a mom knows how. I said and did nothing. Is it ludicrous to choose to believe that he was just doing what kids did? I became really clever at living in denial that my son was developing a problem. After all, I'd started drinking at age thirteen. My son was okay ... until he wasn't. Or so I thought.

In middle school, he won the Best Friend counseling award. But by the time he was in high school, he had a cocaine habit. Every morning of high school, my worst nightmare played out over and over again. Sort of like movie *Groundhog Day*. He yelled, and he cussed, and he stomped each and every morning as I tried to get him out of bed and ready for school. Yet, as he showered, I rewarded his behavior by making his favorite fried egg sandwich to eat as I drove him to school. Since that time, at the age of twenty-four, he has apologized for putting me through all those mornings. Then just the other day, at age twenty-six, he hugged me hard and would not let me go. He said, "Mom, I am so sorry for all I did to you." I replied by hugging him back, even harder, and saying, "Zac, I am so sorry for all I did and did not do to you, but it got us here to this beautiful place. So worth it. Thank you, God, for saving us."

Little did I know, when I dropped him off at school, he walked through the front door and out the back to the ditch behind the school to get high. Some mornings, he even had me drive to the back entrance of the school. "Less traffic," he said. What I was really doing was driving him closer to the ditch so he didn't have to walk all the way through the school to get high. I became the dreaded helicopter mom. No, I had become the perfect helicopter mom. At last I had found perfection. Literally, each morning I would put on my pilot uniform, launch my helicopter, and fly my son to school, first class. All the while thinking I was helping by rescuing him from his all-consuming discomfort. Instead, we were headed for a disastrous crash. No surprise that he failed most classes. The counselor would call us in for meetings, and he promised to try harder. I was divorced and went as a single parent to those meetings. I thought I could love my son enough for both parents. I was sorely mistaken. Things continued to escalate. My son called me, crying from the high school restroom floor to come get him, because he could not take it anymore. I did not know what "it" was. But

I knew it was bad. He had missed so much school; the counselor told me that I had twenty-four hours to withdraw him or I would be arrested for his truancy and be forced to pay a $5,000 fine. Operation rescue was launched.

I arrived at the school counselor's office and signed the paperwork to homeschool him. On my way to get him, I walked past the latest art display in the hallway. A huge display of charcoal and pencil sketches caught my eye, so I went closer. I gasped! To my horror and shock, on display for the whole school to see were at least ten sketches of my son asleep (passed out) on his desk. I could not breathe. I was terrified and paralyzed. I was staring straight at the proof of what was going on with my son, and I had refused to see it. I was so confused and angry. Guess what I did? Nothing. I said nothing. I told no one, not even my son. I did not like to talk about things. I got that part down to *perfection*.

How much more evidence did I need? Well, apparently much more. Because we registered for online homeschool. The police would drop by our house to check his status. I went to work, and he stayed home. He did no school work. I know you must be thinking that we needed counseling, and you are right. This helicopter mom's next mission involved going to see a wonderful Christian counselor, Kelly Zentner. My son and I were not into Jesus at the time, but I had heard she was awesome with teens. I went, and he went, and we went together. I think I was the only one willing to be helped at the time. I know that you cannot force someone to be helped. They need to want to be helped. They need to be ready. I saw a funny saying posted in her office waiting room that inspired me to keep coming back for more counseling. Oh, and make another bumper sticker. "Good morning. This is God. I will be handling all your problems today. I will *not* need your help. Take the day off."

11

We tried Wednesday teen night at church. I would drop my son off. You guessed it … he went in the front door of the church and out the back. He proceeded to vandalize homes in our neighborhood. Our neighborhood was close enough for him to walk the three miles from the church. Something no good was about to go down in my life.

One Wednesday night a man and his son showed up at our house. I will never forget the eerie feeling of evil wash over me as I approached those shadowed figures at my front door. I knew it was bad. Like the dreaded phone call you get in the middle of the night. It is not a good sign. It was a father and his son. The dad told me that they had just seen my son hopping over their fence. I told them that my son was at church. Denial can get so big. The boy at the door responded, "I went to school with your son, and I recognized him." There was a breach in my solid wall of denial. My wall was beginning to leak. The dad also informed me that his other neighbor had been robbed the night before, and he almost shot one of the intruders. I froze in terror. I got in my helicopter and went to look for my son. I found him in the neighborhood in possession of stolen tools. I went to those houses and apologized. My son did not come.

My son began to stay away a week at a time. I was so scared he was dead. The long, slow, painful spiral downward was coming to an end. Homeschooling did not work. I got him into a self-paced high school where he met his girlfriend. One day, the school principal called me to say that my son pulled a knife and threatened to stab himself in the chest because she broke up with him. The principal said that either she was going to call the police or I needed to come take him to a rehabilitation facility. I choppered right over to save him, again. He was admitted to a day treatment program for two weeks and lived with me at night. He was given medication for the psychotic episode. There was a long weekend off for a holiday, and he did cocaine. He thought it would be out of his system before he went back to rehab. They drug tested him twice for accuracy. And then they added chemical dependency issues to his diagnosis. He had to stay longer. They gave him more medications to help him sleep. He tried taking the prescribed antidepressants, but they made him feel foggy. So he quit taking all medications.

After he was discharged, he went to live with a friend because we had ransacked his room for drugs, taken the door off, and threatened to kick him out. I was trying my tough love act at last. Days and weeks would go by, and I would not hear from him. That pain was unbearable. When he did call, I would cry and yell at him for not calling me to let me know where he was and if he was okay. Time for me to go back to counseling. Did I mention, in the middle of all that, I was completing my PhD? Oh, and drinking wine every night at five o'clock, with three other children and a husband at home, a full-time teaching job, and competing in triathlons? How to stay distracted from the obvious. I was striving for perfection. If I could not be the perfect mom, I was going to be perfect at finishing all bottles of wine I opened. I should have gotten the Oscar for my starring role in a movie called *Helicopter Mom* or *Mission Impossible Mom*. Or at least recognized for my contribution to a documentary titled *Perfecting the Art of Drinking*.

So my beautiful Christian counselor, Kelly, asked me this time if I was ready at last to try things her way. I was ready. Best advice I ever got. She asked me what I wanted most from my son. I replied, "I want to know he is alive and safe." So she said, "Next time he calls, ask him over for his favorite dinner. No questions or tears." She explained to me that every time he called and I cried about him not calling, it reinforced him being a failure. He failed at school, boyhood, and being a good son. He later told me he blamed himself for me divorcing his dad. So when I cried and yelled, he felt he failed again. So why bother to try to do better if he was met with failure at every turn. So I began to do things her way.

She never pushed God on me during our sessions. She would just say things like, "I think God is cheering for you from heaven, saying, 'You can do this, Lyn! Just take my hand, and I will take care of you both!'" Since I had been a cheerleader, this made sense to me. So now I am His biggest cheerleading fan. *I go bananas for God!* With peanut butter of course.

However, back then I did not trust God to take care of my son. Kelly had me read *The Shack* (Young 2007). Talk about trust. So I did it her way. It worked. My son came over to eat dinner. My husband, his stepdad, refused to eat with us. He could not stand watching how my son hurt me and I how I just kept trying to love and rescue him. Next time he called, I asked him to do his favorite thing, which was go wakeboarding. I told him I would pay for it and watch him. We did just that. Those were the best of times together.

So we began to do things together that he was good at. A success, not a failure. I could see he was safe and alive, just as Kelly had promised. Did I mention she is amazing? Something slowly started to change in me. I did not know what it was at the time. Kelly said that both she and I would know when it happened. It was like she was opening a small crack in a door and I could just make out a light of something promising on the other side. I convinced my son to at least get his GED. He did. Then he decided to go back to that same self-paced high school to finish his real high school diploma. Do you see the small ray of light too? The door is opening a little wider. Well, he had me fooled as to why he wanted to go back to school. It was for the ex-girlfriend. Or did you already figure that out, and I was the only one in the dark?

At that school, they take your picture the first day you start in your graduation cap and gown as a motivator. The sadness on the face of such a small, lost boy in that picture still haunts me to this day. But it is a great reminder of just how far we have come. One morning, he got up and said to me in passing on his way to the shower, "I think I might be graduating today." At a self-paced school, it happens on a daily basis, and they make an announcement over the loud speaker. Well, I was not going to miss the opportunity to hear his name over the speaker. So I called my husband and ex-husband to come. Both said they could not take off work on such short notice. So I called our best friend Matt who worked at the psychiatric hospital where my son had gone for treatment. And he came to support us. Now that is a best friend. "Operation Love Does," as Bob Goff would say (2012). Did I tell you I used to be the department supervisor of recreation therapists at that very same rehab hospital too?

It came to pass that not too long after his graduation, I got a call from my ex-husband at my work. He told me that our son's ex-girlfriend called him to say that he had threatened to kill himself again. His dad told me he did not believe it was any big deal, but our son was not answering the phone. He was at work and not able to go check on him. So I tried to call our son. I was on the phone outside the building where I taught college. It was a forty-five-minute drive from home, and I was supposed to teach in fifteen minutes. He did not answer. So I did the only thing I knew to do. Call 911. Since I worked in a different city, the police told me they could not help. I had to call the police in the city where my son was. By this time,

I was panic-stricken. What? So I ran inside and went to our administrative assistant. He was so helpful and immediately took charge. He looked up my home city police number and called them to go over and check on him. I will never forget what he did for me that day.

In the meantime, I called Matt again to see if he could go check on my son, as the rehab hospital he worked at was close by our house. He told me later that when he arrived in our driveway, he called his wife, Trish (my BFF), and asked her to pray for him, not knowing what he would find inside. Now those are some best friends. I think Bob Goff is on to something … love does. So Matt went inside to find my son hysterical, punching holes in his closet door. He told him that the police were on their way to see if he needed to go to the hospital. My son got even more upset. I got a call from Matt when the police arrived, and he assured me he would stay with my son till I got home and sent the police on their way.

My ray of light on the other side of the door began to fade. The guilt and shame of being an awful mother had tracked me down. I could not even get a suicide response call right. I had failed once again. It was then I decided it was time to hang up my pilot uniform. My flying machine was tired. I needed a parachute. Time to abort all rescue missions. I knew it was over. I made another counseling appointment for us both. We went back to wakeboarding, and he actually was hired to work there for a while, till he got fired for sleeping (passed out) on the job. Later, they took another chance on him and offered him a job as a summer camp counselor, and he did very well teaching kids to wake and skateboard. I am still connected professionally and personally (so is my son) to that wonderful place and family who gave my son a second chance.

Here comes the unraveling …

Go Bananas for God with Peanut Butter Cupcakes

(Makes 16 cupcakes or 56 minis)

Cupcake Ingredients:
1 1/4 cups unbleached all-purpose flour
1/4 teaspoon salt
1 1/2 teaspoons baking powder
1/2 teaspoon baking soda
1/2 cup sour cream (room temperature)
1 1/2 teaspoons vanilla extract
2 very ripe bananas, diced
1/8 cup brown sugar
1 stick unsalted butter (softened)
3/4 cup granulated sugar
2 large egg yolks (room temperature)
2 large egg whites (room temperature)

Fluffy Banana Filling:
1 box instant banana pudding
1 1/2 cups heavy whipping cream
1/2 cup milk
1/4 cup sour cream

Peanut Butter Frosting:
1/2 cup heavy whipping cream
1 stick unsalted butter softened
12 ounces cream cheese (softened)
1 teaspoon vanilla extract
1 cup peanut butter
1 1/4 cups powder sugar

Garnish and Toppers:
16 toothpicks
16 mini monkey stickers
16 pre-typed small signs cut to size
1/2 cup salted peanuts or banana chips

Directions:

Cupcakes:
- Preheat oven to 325 degrees F. Line cupcake tins with yellow color-stay papers.
- In medium bowl, combine flour, salt, baking powder, and baking soda.
- In small bowl mix, sour cream and vanilla and set aside.
- Mix bananas with brown sugar in sauté pan; heat over medium heat till bubbles. Set aside to slightly cool.
- In electric mixer, combine butter and sugar. Add egg yolks. Mix on medium high till fluffy.
- Whip both egg whites in small bowl with wire whisk till frothy then add to butter and sugar. Combine thoroughly.
- Lower mixer speed to lowest setting. Alternate between banana, sour cream, and dry ingredients in two portions slowly to mixer just till combined.
- Bake 15–20 minutes and cool completely.

Filling:
- In electric mixer, whip pudding, heavy whipping cream, milk, and sour cream till fluffy.
- Place in piping bag.
- Cut hole in center of cupcakes and fill with pudding mixture.

Frosting:
- In electric mixer on high, whip heavy cream till fluffy. Scoop into separate bowl and set aside.
- In same electric mixer on medium high, beat butter, cream cheese, vanilla extract.
- Add peanut butter and powdered sugar on low and mix thoroughly.
- Fold in whip cream just till well blended.
- Put in piping bag. Frost cupcakes.

Garnish and Topper:
- Cut out small sayings and monkey sticker.
- Use glue gun to adhere to top of toothpick.
- Garnish with salted peanuts or banana chip.

CHAPTER 3

I NEED S'MORE GOD'S LOVE

Did I mention I hate answering the phone? My experience answering has not left me with a strong desire to pick up. I prefer to call people back. Just in case I need to prepare for bad news. Well, I was not prepared for this one. I saw a missed call and message from my ex-husband. As I listened, he told me that he had just picked our son up outside jail. He spent the night there after being arrested for possession of marijuana. So I did the only thing I knew to do, put on my pilot uniform and launch a lawyer-to-the-rescue mission! The lawyer got him two years' probation. But my son could not adhere to the terms. He was so depressed. I knew he needed to get out of here, away from his "bad" friends. It must be the friends' fault, right? It is still a mystery to me what I chose to believe and see.

That said, I came up with a great idea that he should go to Colorado for the winter and be a ski lift operator and snowboard every day. He got the job and left for Colorado with one of his friends. One night, his lawyer called him for his probation hearing that was scheduled for eight o'clock the next morning. Now he was in Colorado, with no way to get a flight on time to make the hearing. A warrant was issued for his arrest. Why did I not think to hop in my helicopter and fly him home?

It is going to get worse before it gets better. While he was still in Colorado, he shattered his elbow jumping off a cliff on his snowboard. I never had the guts to ask him if he was high when the accident occurred. He had emergency surgery. Funny thing, he had his buddies help walk him off the mountain because the emergency helicopter was $10,000 for a ride off the mountain to the hospital. I would have picked him up for free in my helicopter. They did the surgery. Did you already guess that he was uninsured at the time? They released him home right after recovery, all drugged up on pain killers, alone on a bus. My safe-and-alive radar was on high alert. I could not reach him. I called his apartment manager and asked her to go check on him to see if he was okay. She could not find him. Seriously, this really happened. I am not making this up. The scene that was unfolding was filled with a relentless, desperate attempt to find my son. I was not sure I could do this ... be so far away and unable to help him. That's when I suddenly knew we were headed to the bottom. *Please let this be it. His bottom.* For now, all I could do was wait. What a scary enterprise.

Let me be clear about one thing. Waiting is the hardest part. When I did reach him, he wanted me to come get him. No one would help me on the home front. My husband and my ex were out on this mission. So I called my sister Cathy (aka Gina) in Wyoming to meet me in Denver. She lovingly dropped everything and drove me up to Aspen so I could drive my son in his car back home to Texas. Now that is a big sister for you. Operation Love Does again.

Upon our return to Texas, my son got his own new "pot" lawyer. Luckily, the first lawyer was known for giving short court notices to his clients, so the warrant was dismissed. I begged my son to do community service with me. I did a lot of volunteer work with many nonprofit community organizations with my college students. He did. I enjoyed that time with him. He is so gifted and compassionate with people who have disabilities. I hoped that maybe the judge would be lenient when he saw my son's good deeds. But as the court date got closer, fear was gnawing away at me. I not only had nightmares but also daymares of my son going to jail and being raped and beaten. I was coming undone. I was going to counseling every week so Kelly could help prepare me for the worst fear of my life coming true—not being able to save my son.

Through continued counseling, I had begun to see and feel different. Kelly kept telling me that God was just waiting for me to let go of my need to control my son's life and trust Him. I was so busy trying to be the *perfect* mom. I had been playing God all these years. My son did not even know about God. He only knew to cry out to me. How could he be hungry for God when I fed him all his needs? I got in the way of him crying out to God (D'Arcy 1996). I truly believe that is why God got me out of the way. I had to quit letting my *ego* get in the way because I was *e*dging *G*od *o*ut. My biggest obstacle in all of this was myself. Get out of your own way!

On the morning of my son's sentencing, he came down stairs in five layers of clothes because he said jail was cold. I did not bother to tell him that they had their own style of clothing for him and it came in black-and-white stripes or bright orange. Here's what's strange. I realized that I was walking my son straight toward my biggest fear. Holding his hand, no less.

We arrived at the courthouse and were waiting on a bench in the hallway when I witnessed my first miracle. I saw a vision of Jesus reflected in the Plexiglas window across from us. I am not kidding. I saw Jesus sitting next to us on the bench. My counselor had encouraged me to keep a journal, and I had begun drawing illustrations of what I was experiencing. There He was waiting with us. Waiting for me to give my son back. After all, He had only loaned him to me. So there I was sitting between my son and God the Father's son, Jesus. I did not miss the irony of this vision. And I hope you don't either.

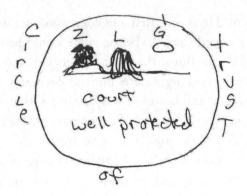

Journal sketch, "Plexiglas Vision Waiting for Sentencing with Jesus."

My son started to cry and said he did not want me to go in the courtroom to see him handcuffed. I said okay. I was sure that I would have screamed. And as we hugged good-bye, he whispered in my ear that he was not clean. There was nothing left to say. It took only a few minutes, and his lawyer came out and said, "He is gone." The biggest tear of my life rolled down my cheek.

Journal sketch, "Biggest Tear I Ever Cried."

At that moment, I felt like I got sucker punched in the gut. I felt the air leave my body, and I staggered backward. I asked the lawyer what to do now, and he said call the jail and see when visiting hours were. I asked, "How long did he get?" He got one hundred days. Every time I read this

section, the tears start to well up in my eyes again and again and again …
I will never forget the day I got out of God's way. Or should I say God got
me out of His way … to my son.

So I went to my car and called my husband and my ex-husband with
the news and drove home. Will you think I am nuts if I tell you that Jesus
was in my passenger seat? I felt His presence. I could also sense the figure
of an angel flying over the top of my car, dressed in a long white robe
with wings, his long white hair flowing in the wind, emanating radiance.
Was this my guardian angel? I had no idea what to do next. Just go home?
Everything felt different. What was I supposed to do now? Where is the
book on what to do the day your son goes to jail? I mean seriously. There
are so many books on just about every DIY project you can imagine. But
where was the book about what I was supposed to do for the next hundred
days? I would soon learn there is a book. It is called the Bible.

I pulled in my driveway, and the phone rang. You guessed it. At last the
Born Again Birthday phone call, May 18, 2011. His one phone call from
jail. He was beside himself crying. The guard had to try to get him to calm
down to talk to me. All I could think about was how my handsome son
would be raped or beaten or both. But out of my mouth came these very
words: "You need to visualize yourself surrounded by a suit of armor. With
a shield and helmet. That will be God protecting you. Now pull yourself
together and stop crying. You have to be strong. I will be there to see you
as soon as I can." The guard told me visiting hours were Saturday. This
was Wednesday. How would I survive till then? How would he survive
without me? I hung up and began to wail in mourning. I felt like my son
had died. God had gotten me out of his way.

I ran to my neighbor Theresa N., and she comforted me. She was so
kind just to hold me and let me cry. She just listened. I will never forget her
gift that day. Then I walked back home and noticed on my front porch a
party bag with the name *Jesus* on it. Inside was my very first Bible. It was
from my dear friend Stephanie W., who is a beautiful, strong Christian
woman. She had put several quotes on a card in there for me to read. I
know now they are called scripture passages, not quotes. She had written
the addresses. The first one I looked up was Ephesians 6: 10—17, *The
Armor of God* (NKJV). I hit my knees and gave my life to Jesus. I was
reborn at that very moment. My second miracle had occurred. I was saved

by Jesus. How did I know those words before in the car on the phone with my son? There is only one answer … God. God had given me those words. God had given me a sign that He would protect and care for my son. He was the only one who could save us. I called my friend to thank her and said I was so scared to see my son behind bars. I thought I might faint, cry, and scream. I did not know how I would handle it. She told me that when I went to visit him to visualize angels surrounding us. One in front, one behind, and one on each side. I had finally learned to trust God. I didn't need my helicopter for rescue missions anymore.

All I needed was my angels and *s'more God's love.*

I Need S'more God's Love Cupcakes

(Makes 18 cupcakes)

Cupcake Ingredients:
1 1/2 cups unbleached all-purpose flour
1/2 cup dark cocoa powder
1/2 teaspoon salt
1 1/2 teaspoons baking soda

Room temperature:
1 cup buttermilk
1/2 cup sour cream
1/4 cup brewed coffee
2 teaspoons vanilla extract
1 1/2 sticks unsalted butter
2/3 cup granulated sugar
2/3 cup brown sugar
2 extra-large eggs
4 ounces melted dark chocolate

Ganache Filling:
8 ounces dark chocolate chips
1 cup heavy whipping cream
1 tablespoon unsalted butter

Marshmallow Fluff:
4 egg whites
2 teaspoon vanilla
2 cups granulated sugar
1/2 teaspoon crème of tartar
4 1/2 ounces water

Garnish and Toppers:
1 package graham crackers (about 8)
27 toothpicks
18 mini marshmallows
18 pre-typed small signs cut to size

Directions:
- Preheat oven to 350 degrees F. Line cupcake tins with color-stay papers.
- In medium bowl, combine flour, coco powder, salt, and baking soda.
- In small bowl, combine buttermilk, sour cream, coffee, and vanilla.
- In electric mixer, combine butter and both sugars. Add one egg at a time. Mix on medium high till fluffy.
- Lower mixer speed to lowest setting. Alternating between wet and dry ingredients in two portions, slowly add to mixer.
- Melt dark chocolate in microwave-safe bowl (30–60 seconds).
- Add melted chocolate. Mix only till all ingredients are incorporated. Do not over mix.
- Bake for 15 minutes and cool completely.

Filling:
- Heat heavy whipping cream to simmer in small pan on stove.
- Place dark chocolate chips in a microwave-safe bowl.
- Pour heated cream over chocolate, add butter, and let stand one minute. Stir till thoroughly combined.
- Let cool and place in piping bag.
- Cut hole in center of cupcakes and fill with ganache mixture.

Fluff:
- In electric mixer on high, beat egg whites and vanilla till stiff peaks form.
- In small pan over medium high heat, combine sugar, crème of tartar, and water. Bring to boil and slowly drizzle down side of mixing bowl into whipped egg mixture till completely blended.
- Put in piping bag and form peaks on cupcake.
- Optional: toast top under broiler in oven. Be careful not to burn.

Garnish and Topper:
- Crush five graham crackers in plastic bag by smashing with rolling pin. Sprinkle over frosting.
- Break up three of the crackers into half-size pieces. These do not need to be uniform in size. Stick on top of cupcake.

- Cut nine of the toothpicks in half. Skewer the mini marshmallows on whole toothpick and insert half toothpicks through marshmallow so it looks like a cross.
- Cut out small sayings. Use glue gun to adhere to top of toothpick.

CHAPTER 4

ASK, ACCEPT, AND
LIVE FORGIVEN

Did you know when you go see someone in jail they have to put your name on their visitation list? In my son's jail, you could only have five people on the list. All persons on the list had to arrive and register together at the same time in order to share the twenty-minute visitation, only then to decide how to split up the twenty-minute timeslot. So my ex-husband was on the list with me. During our marriage, we had fought and yelled a lot when we spoke to each other. How were we going to see him together? Are you kidding me? I had wanted the divorce. I also felt guilty that in doing so I had damaged our son. I wore the bad mother guilt and shame like a hundred-pound weight on my back. I carried it everywhere with me (along with my box or jug of wine of course).

So I called my older sister Cathy, who had helped me get my son back from his Colorado accident, and asked her what to do. She asked me, "Have you thought of just calling your ex and asking him to put your differences aside for your son and go see him in jail with you?" Well, that was a radical notion. No, I hadn't thought of that. Just as I hung up with her, before I lost my courage, I called him. I said, "Before you hang up or say anything, I want to apologize for my role in the failure of our marriage and anything I did that affected the predicament that our son was in. Will you forgive me and go see him with me in jail?" And he simply replied, "Yes." Okay, that is not how I expected that to go. No arguing, yelling, name-calling, or hanging up on each other. Just one simple word … yes. *This is a good start*, I thought. I just stared at my cell phone in disbelief, as it lay cradled in my hand. *He said yes.* Miracle number three had occurred.

The inexplicable power of forgiveness. Until that day, I had never encountered honest-to-goodness forgiveness. It doesn't matter if the other person doesn't forgive you, because forgiveness is not about the other person. It is about yourself. All you need to do is experience it one time, and you will know exactly what I am talking about. The power is in the asking. Asking from an honest, true place. That day, I had not only asked for forgiveness from my ex-husband but also from God. I was asking God to forgive my trespasses as He forgives us. What I realized next was the acceptance part. I had to accept my ex-husband's and God's forgiveness. The even bigger part … drum roll please … was then to live it. The hardest part of asking my ex for forgiveness was not the asking part. It was forgiving myself for my part that led my son down that destructive path to jail. And then to live a life of forgiveness. If we do not live forgiven, then others can't see what that looks like. I am not even sure what it looks like, but I know it when I feel and see it. That's where I need to go. If we live forgiven, wear forgiveness, talk forgiveness, look forgiven, then others will forgive themselves. It is our gift to the world. Can you imagine if we all walked around living a life of forgiveness? No need for war. What if we put down our weapons and say to one another, "I am sorry. Please forgive me for my part in our misunderstanding." Jesus died on the cross a horrific death so that all, and I mean *all*, our sins would be forgiven. So if He did that for us, can't we simply apologize so others will heal? And we heal ourselves?

Part of the twelve-step recovery program, steps 5–10, is about making amends. I was beginning those steps before I had ever heard or read about them. Somehow, the part about asking God and others I had wronged to forgive me became my new endeavor. It took me till my fifty-first birthday to ask my son to forgive me for not trying to stop him from using drugs way back when he was thirteen and passed out on our lawn. I told him that I had been drinking since the age of thirteen, and my parents never tried to stop me either. I had repeated that pattern with him as a parent. But I am breaking the pattern now with this apology. You see, when you live forgiven, you free up a huge part of your time and soul to do so many other things that bring joy to you and others. And time to bake *fudgy brownie cupcakes about forgiveness,* and do yoga of course. More on yoga later.

Back to jail visitation. Now, if you have never been inside a jail, it is just like on TV or in the movies. After you register to visit, they call out the inmates' numbers. My son's number was R1. As the cell doors to the visiting area slide open, the inmates walk with hands behind their backs and sit behind the Plexiglas. More magic Plexiglas. You sit down across from them, and you both pick up your phones. He was in his stripes.

Journal sketch, "Angels in Jail."

So here I am again looking into a Plexiglas window, and I see the wings of angels reflected behind him and me. What is it with me connecting to

Jesus through Plexiglas windows? Got to be something symbolic there. But there they were, those angels that my friend Stephanie W. told me to surround myself with. I called upon them as I walked in. And there they were. I felt so safe, calm, and peaceful. How was this miracle possible? There is only one answer. God. Capital T R U S T. Miracle number four had arrived. I put my hand up on the Plexiglas and told him to put his hand across from mine. He sobbed how sorry he was and told me it was not my fault and that I was a good mother. But how does being a good mother reconcile with what I was seeing behind that Plexiglas? My son was an inmate, and I was partly responsible for that. I was not a good mother. I told him his dad and brother was there to see him too. He looked so relieved. Forgiveness is so Big! That face he was wearing is what forgiveness looks like. I have seen it now. I have proof. Or anyway, that's how it felt.

I must tell you something here. My ex and I had a very tenuous discussion about who should go in to see our son first. If you haven't figured out by now, I am a very emotional person. If you ever meet me, you will see everything I feel on my face. My ex did not want me to freak our son out with my scared face. But as we were talking, I saw something in my ex-husband's face that I had never seen before … fear. So I offered to go first for my turn, with a solemn promise that I would be calm and be there to support, not scare, him. After, I realized this really wasn't about me at all. It was about a father and son needing so badly to forgive each other and heal. And I was not going it alone. I had my angels going with me.

When my visitation turn was over, I walked out, and across the waiting room, sitting on the chair was my pale, scared-to-death ex-husband. The anticipation on his face as to what my face would look like was palpable. His eyes were staring straight into mine with a desperate plea of *please let him be okay!* The angels guided me over to him. He stood up, and I hugged him with my angel wings. I whispered to him, "He's okay. He's okay. He is just so happy you are here to see him." I have never in my life reassured someone with such empathy before. You see, it is our job as parents to love our kids. That's why we were put here. Even if we are ruined. That's the divine secret of parenthood. To come here to this place, you must demonstrate unconditional love.

So the next Sunday, I went up to a church close by (the same church my son pretended to go to those Wednesday nights long ago). I went in and wept through the service. On the way out, I saw a pamphlet on codependency courses they offered. I took one. Thus began a yearlong quest on how to let my son go. It was an amazing journey filled with Christian codependency workbooks and Jesus. I told you I was a straight-A student. I had potential to get this thing right. I ran hard at God; the *perfectionist* in me was still trying so hard to get it right. I started attending that church twice on Sundays. I could not get enough of His word. I called it my double-header Sundays. It was father and son preachers who gave sermons back to back. I went to both sermons and sang my heart out. When they called people to the altar to pray, I didn't just walk up there like everyone else, I ran. I celebrated my Born Again Birthday by getting baptized June 26, 2011. Happy birthday to me!

My baptism was one of the best days of my life. I was somehow freeing myself from the chains of codependency, addiction, and the need to be the *perfect* mother. Every chain has two sides. What's on the other side of your chain? I even filled a small bottle with the baptism water when they weren't looking so I could keep it. I still have it in an old perfume bottle of my mom's. I grew up Catholic and was baptized as a baby but spent most of my adult life running away from God. Now I was running to God. We were somehow now in a field of flowers together, holding hands during my son's jail time. It dawned on me. If God could be a good father to me, an alcoholic daughter, then perhaps I could be a good mother to my son.

I am not going to pretend driving and seeing my son behind bars for a hundred days of summer was easy. But it was okay. I was no longer alone. God and my angels went everywhere with me. You know, I used to judge parents of kids in jail. Till I sat in that waiting room outside his cell looking around at all the wives, mothers, girlfriends, and kids and said to myself, "Well, Lyn, go ahead and toss the first stone." My son got moved to a tougher jail and put in a cell with eighteen men with big tattoos. I tried not to freak out. He said he felt the *armor and God* protecting him, as many situations that could have gone very badly did not.

The day he was released, my stepdaughter, my ex, and his son all went to pick him up. We all sat together, this perfectly broken blended family, waiting for those cell doors to open. I was so nervous. I will never forget my stepdaughter Sam sitting their holding my hand and whispering in my ear, "He is gonna be in shock when he walks out, so don't freak him out and run at him." But all I could think about was Luke 15, the prodigal son story (NKJV). And yes, as those bars slid open and he stepped out with his brown paper R1 sack, I ran at him. Picked him up and hugged him. I had heard about the prodigal son story. But I never remember anyone mentioning that the father ran to his son. Well, this mother ran to her son. My son was twenty-one at the time but looked thirteen. Due to his drug use, he had lost those seven years. He was a frail, small, young boy again. It would get worse before it got better. But I'm gonna get sober soon. Get ready; my third birthday is coming up.

God never left my side. I read my Bible every morning with my coffee. My husband got me a coffee mug with a picture of Jesus on it so I could have coffee with Jesus in the mornings. One day my son peeked his head down the stairs as I was reading with Jesus, and he asked me, "Mom, are you where you want to be when Jesus comes?" And I answered, "Yes!" without even thinking about it. I had surrendered my life to God. He had shown me what it meant to give up your son only to get him back again. I read about Abraham and his son Isaac in Genesis 22. Where God asked him to sacrifice his son for Him. The ultimate act of surrender of your son. Just like God surrendering His son, Jesus, for us. I get that. I surrendered my son to God too. How can all those stories written thousands of years ago in the Bible still be happening today? It's as true today as back then. I used to think that people finding Jesus in jail was a bunch of hooey. Till it happened to me and my son. We found Jesus on both sides of those bars. Why is it you don't get things till they happen to you? At least now I don't just remember all the bad things but the joyful ones as well.

I am not sure what my family was thinking about me during my transformation. Or for that matter, what they think of me today. It was like I was in a big field divided by a white picket fence. I was on one side running with Jesus. My son was watching and walking along to see what would happen next. He was liking this new mom. He told me that I was easier to talk to, easier to be around, and easier to love. My husband was on the other side of the fence, watching me and coming over every once in a while before going back. I began to give my testimony to Christian college groups, and my husband heard me speak for the first time. He told the group that he had witnessed me being reborn. And that he wanted what I had but was not willing to do what I had done to get it. He had started going to church with me, but my husband is very slow to change. He is evolving at his own pace, on his own journey with God.

I asked my husband one time, "Do you think that I am weird going to church all the time?" He said, "No, I can see it brings you great comfort." I thought he would leave me for becoming a born-again Christian. By the way, I used to think they were weird ... till I became one. I love being weird. I just love Jesus! I am a Jesus junky for sure. I am just so proud to be God's daughter. I never felt worthy before. However, during this whole time, I was still drinking every night to cope. Wine in a box had become not only my five o'clock habit but my new sleeping pill. I had crossed the line into alcoholism.

But I am about to cross another line ... into recovery.

Forgiveness Fudgy Brownie Cupcakes

(*Gluten-free; makes 16 cupcakes)

Cupcake Ingredients:
1 stick unsalted butter
8 ounces chopped dark chocolate
1/4 cup granulated sugar
3/4 cup light brown sugar
2 large eggs
1/4 cup brewed coffee
1/2 cup gluten-free baking flour
1/4 cup dark cocoa powder
3/4 teaspoon coarse kosher salt
1 teaspoon coarse kosher salt to sprinkle on top

Filling:
1 (12-ounce) can raspberry pastry filling

Frosting:
1/2 cup heavy whipping cream
8 ounces softened cream cheese
1 teaspoon vanilla extract
a pinch of salt
1/3 cup powder sugar

Garnish and Toppers:
16 store-bought chalkboard toothpick toppers
16 "Ask, Accept, and Live Forgiven" sayings

Directions:
- Preheat oven to 350 degrees F. Line cupcake pan with color-stay papers or spray.
- In medium microwave-safe bowl, melt butter and chopped dark chocolate together in microwave on 50 percent power for 30 seconds Take out and mix. Heat longer in 10-second increments till fully melted and mixed.
- Combine sugar and brown sugar into one measuring cup. Do not pack the brown sugar. Keep it loose.
- Add the combined cup of sugar and then eggs one at a time to mixer.
- Add coffee, flour, cocoa powder, and salt. Mix till blended thoroughly. Do not over mix.
- Hold hand high above cupcake to avoid over-salting and lightly sprinkle course kosher salt on top of each cupcake.
- Bake for 20 minutes or till toothpick comes out clean. Cool completely.

Filling:
- Fill piping bag with raspberry pastry filling.
- Pipe center of top of brownie with raspberry pastry filling.

Frosting:
- In electric mixer on high, whip heavy cream till it peaks. Scoop into small bowl. Set aside.
- In same mixer, beat cream cheese, vanilla, salt, and powder sugar on low speed till blended.
- Fold in whip cream just till blended.
- Put in piping bag and frost outer rim of brownie outside the raspberry center.
- Add another dollop of raspberry to center of frosting.

Garnish and Topper:
- Cut out sayings. Use glue gun to adhere to top of store-bought chalkboard toothpick toppers.

CHAPTER 5

LET GOD ALTER YOUR MOOD

Every poor decision I made was under the influence of alcohol. Until the last one—my decision to get sober. It took over an entire year from the time my son went to jail to get sober. I was finally ready. I will never forget that day. It was Father's Day, and I was celebrating with one of my favorite men, my eighty-one-year-old dad. I was drinking my flipflop bottle of wine. How can wine be bad for you if it comes in a bottle decorated with cute flip-flops? Tricky alcohol. I caught a glimpse of myself reflected in our sliding glass door (kind of like the Plexiglas window images). And I was stunned by what I saw. I saw an alcoholic. I set my wine glass down. Walked upstairs. Turned on my computer. And Googled AA. I found a group called Serendipity. I liked the name. Perhaps I would find a beautiful surprise there. It was only Sunday. The group did not meet till the following Tuesday at 11:00 a.m. Not sure why or how I stayed sober all day Monday. Because I drank wine and beer almost every day for the past thirty years. God was performing a modern-day miracle here. By my count, this is miracle number five.

I did not tell my dad or husband I was going to go to AA. I was afraid they would talk me out of it. After all, I did not want to ruin our daily five o'clock happy hour together. So on Tuesday, June 18, 2012, I celebrated my third birthday. The *sober one*. By showing up at Serendipity. Do you believe it was right next door to a bar? Literally, an adjoining wall connected the two buildings in a small rundown strip mall. I thought that when I went in I would see a bunch of bums, haggard and beaten down. But you know what I saw? People who looked just like me. Serendipitous, wouldn't you say?

If you have never been to a meeting, at the beginning they ask who is a newcomer. I raised my hand. Big mistake! They aimed the whole meeting at me. I tried to melt in my chair and get smaller under the table so as not to be so noticeable. No dice. After the meeting, a woman came up to me and asked if I had a *Big Book*. I said no ... not even sure what it was. So she bought me the *Big Book of AA* (Smith and Wilson 2001) and put her name, Karen, and phone number inside. She would later become my sponsor. I mentioned to her that no one knew I had come to the meeting, and I had no plans to tell anyone. She told me that AA is an honest program, and I needed to at least tell my husband.

So I went home and anxiously waited for my husband to come home from work. We were supposed to go out to dinner with family and friends that evening (which of course would involve drinking). I did not go anywhere that alcohol was not served. I had found another meeting up at our church that night and knew I needed to go. So when he came home, this inexplicable strange calmness came over me. I told him that I thought I was an alcoholic. That I had attended my first AA meeting that morning, and I needed to go to another meeting that night up at church. He asked me, "What about dinner?" I told him, "I am not going to be able to go." He said, "You are not an alcoholic. You don't drink in the morning." I told him, "I have been trying to quit by myself for a while on and off the past year and could not do it." So he went to dinner without me.

Here are a few things I tried in an effort to control my drinking. Just drinking on weekends. Well, by Sunday night I would say to myself (as a poured a glass of wine in my cute sparkly glass), "It is still the weekend." Then I added Thursday night back. Because in my college days, I recalled weekends began on Thursdays. Pretty soon, I added Monday through Wednesday back to my "controlled drinking schedule." But I would limit myself to the medically recommended one to two glasses of wine a day. So I just invested in really large wine glasses. Then I switched from wine in a bottle to a box with the soda shop spigot. How can wine with a fun pour spout be bad for you? Felt childlike and harmless. Or so I told myself. Plus, I could not see through the cardboard box as I drained it. Man, I was really good at selling lies to myself. I needed to go to that church meeting to at least see if I was an alcoholic or not. So I went.

They offered me a twenty-four-hour chip. I accepted. I was not really sure what it was exactly. Till I asked. They told me it meant that I had an honest desire to not drink for the next twenty-four hours. Well, since I had not drunk on Monday, and it was already 7:00 p.m. on Tuesday, I could probably do that. As I write these words, after just celebrating year four of sobriety, I realize I did not have a drinking problem; I had a thinking problem. God was and still is doing for me what I could not do for myself. Stay sober. He took my craving and replaced it with a craving for Him. As I look back at those years and the time elapsed since then, I am just amazed how different my thoughts are and how far I have come. I don't think about drinking anymore on a regular basis (besides my husband's drinking of course). Just like the nine-step promises say in AA, "Our whole attitude and outlook upon life will change. We will suddenly realize that God is doing for us what we could not do for ourselves" (Smith and Wilson 2001, 84). Can I get an amen?

I am happy, joyous, and free ... well most of the time anyway. It used to bother me when I read in the bible from Galatians 5: 22–23 about the Holy Spirit filling our lives with "love, peace, patience, kindness, goodness, faithfulness, gentleness, and self-control" (NKJV). I had been missing the self-control part concerning drinking wine. I laughed when I read Ephesians 5:18, "Don't be drunk on wine, because it will ruin your life. Instead, be filled with the Holy Spirit" (NKJV). God has a sense of humor. I told you there was a book on what to do the day your son went to jail. But there are two books on how to live your life sober. One based on the Bible, *Big Book of AA* (Smith and Wilson 2001), and God's love story for addicts called *The Life Recovery Bible* (Arterburn and Stoop 1998). Both were given to me by someone in AA. So I made a promise to God, that if I ever met someone who needed one, I would buy it for them. I have bought five so far and have given it to others who struggle with addiction. I just recently loaned mine to my husband.

What I really love about my Salvation and Sober Birthdays is that I chose them. I chose God. I chose life without alcohol. That first day in AA, I asked God to take my craving, and He did. I have not once in all four years of sobriety craved a drink. I realize I no longer need wine to alter my mood. *I need a mini mood pie cupcake.* And of course some bumper stickers.

I will admit living sober in a drinking world has been met with some challenges. Year one, I think my dad and husband were angry they lost their happy hour drinking buddy. I had to ask them several times not to drink around me. I would go in another room, and they would come join me. My husband would say, "You don't love me anymore." Now he was drinking when he said those words. I learned in AA to wait till he was not drinking to talk to him about it. So I would wait till morning and ask my dad and husband to please honor my decision to not come around me while drinking or after drinking. Perhaps they were missing my company during that time of the day we usually spent together. I mean, why should they have to give it up just because I had a problem? I get that. My first-year anniversary birthday of being sober was toasted with scotch-whiskey and beer by my husband and dad.

I began to get creative during the drinking hour. I started baking cupcakes. I needed to stay busy and put something in my hands. I never baked before but had begun watching the Cooking Channel and decided to try my hand at baking cupcakes. I loved the show "Cupcake Wars"

(Television Food Network 2016). I still watch it today and think about going on there sometime. Maybe a competition for the national AA convention? Hmmm … I'm just sayin'. I invited a twenty-two-year-old comedian and author, Kevin Breel (2015), from Canada to come speak at our university about his new book and experience with suicide and depression. You should check him out. The one message he hoped to pass to us was to "own your own story." His counselor told him you have two choices. You can share your story or be ashamed of your story. Guess which one I picked? I also made cupcakes and bumper stickers for the event with all his quotes from his book.

So I began making cupcakes at five o'clock instead of drinking. I "baked" my way through happy hour (get it?). I experimented with unique flavor names as homage to God. I even made high-heel shoe cupcakes, since I was taking one step at a time. I crack my own self up. I would take cupcakes to AA with me. I put sayings on toothpick toppers that said "One Step at a Time; I Have a Thinking Problem; Addicted to God; Remain Teachable; HALT; High on Hope; Anger is One Letter Away from *D*anger." I became known as the cupcake lady. I started bringing them to my college classes too. I felt like a kindergarten teacher bringing sweet treats for her kids. I realized it was me who felt like a kid again. Cupcakes make kids happy. I had lost some years of my childhood drinking at such a young age, and I was getting those back. One cupcake at a time.

I also began inventing more bumper stickers for my car. It was time to out myself. I guess my son outed himself too when I asked him to help me write this book. What a courageous act of kindness. You amaze me, son. We just talked the other day about how when he has kids his children will be the first to grow up without a drinking parent. Or grandparent for that matter. We broke the cycle. Miracle number six rocks! I am crying again. Tears of joy this time.

I think what was happening to me was a strong desire to not live in shame and secrecy anymore. Just like Kevin Breel said. AA is anonymous, which I totally get. I wouldn't have gone to that first or subsequent meetings if it had not been confidential. Yet, I don't want to hide in secrecy and promote shame. If I keep my sobriety a secret, that is what I feel like I am doing. So my car has become my mobile billboard for sobriety and God. My cupcakes and my stickers are my way to share my *not so* secret, sober,

Christian life. I even put my *sober birthdate* on my third-year bumper sticker.

Just the other day, I was getting my oil changed. The guy who was working on my car asked me to wait after he was done so he could read all my stickers. He pointed to every one of them as he read. I had a college student drop by my office and ask if the car in the parking lot with all the stickers was mine. I said yes. He said, "I think I have a problem with alcohol." I said, "Come on in." God sure does work in mysterious ways.

My husband takes my car every once in a while. He says he can see people behind him at stoplights reading my stickers. Have you ever been able to drive up behind a car stopped at a light and *not* read its bumper stickers? I don't think it can be done. God is my driver now. I am His passenger. My creativity continues to grow. One night, I even dreamt my first Christian joke. I got up and drew it. I had no idea I had a sense of humor too. I guess being sober brings out one's creativity. I have all this untapped energy. It took a lot of energy to make sure I had enough wine to drink to support my daily habit. Even more energy to keep all my feelings inside. Keep my secrets hidden. Keep my shame alive. Not anymore.

Journal sketch, "My First Christian Joke."

Something clicked. What if I took all that energy and talent I had been using in trying to achieve *perfect* helicopter mom status, *perfect* drinker status, *perfect* teacher status, and put that to use in just being God's *not so perfect* daughter? What if I just let others see and hear God in whatever I say and do? OMG, I think that is it! All this time, God was just waiting for me to connect all the dots.

And then He drew another dot and connected me to yoga.

Peanut Butter and Black Chocolate Mini Mood Pie Cupcakes

(Makes 50 minis)

Cupcake Ingredients:
mini cupcake or push-pop pan
1 1/2 pounds sugar
4 ounces black (or dark) coco powder
15 ounces all-purpose flour
1 1/2 teaspoons baking powder
1 1/2 teaspoons baking soda
1/2 teaspoon salt
4 eggs (room temperature)
1 1/2 cups buttermilk (room temperature)
3 ounces vegetable oil
1 teaspoon vanilla extract
1 1/2 cups hot coffee

Peanut Butter Filling:
4 ounces heavy whipping cream
4 ounces unsalted butter softened
8 ounces cream cheese softened
1/2 teaspoon vanilla extract
6 ounces peanut butter
6 ounces powder sugar
1/4 teaspoon coarse kosher salt

Marshmallow Fluff:
3 egg whites
1 teaspoon vanilla extract
1 cup sugar
3/4 teaspoon cream of tartar
2.5 ounces water

Toppers:
50 toothpicks
50 emoji stickers or
pre-purchased emoji rice paper

Directions:

- Preheat oven to 350 degrees F. Line cupcake tins with mini papers or use baking spray.
- In electric mixer, combine sugar, coco powder, flour, baking powder, baking soda, and salt.
- Add eggs one at a time.
- Add buttermilk, oil, vanilla, and coffee.
- Mix only till all ingredients are incorporated. Do not overmix.
- Fill mini cupcake liners 3/4 full.
- Bake for 5 minutes or till toothpick comes out clean. Cool completely.
- Remove from cupcake paper. Cut cupcake tops off. (Save bottoms for another baking project. Freeze.)
- Select fresh cupcake papers, place one cupcake top in the bottom of each one, top side down. Pair each one up with another cupcake top to add after filling is placed in middle.

Peanut Butter Filling:

- In electric mixer on high, whip heavy cream till fluffy. Scoop into separate bowl and set aside.
- In same electric mixer on medium high, beat butter, cream cheese, and vanilla.
- Add peanut butter and powdered sugar on low and mix thoroughly.
- Add whip cream just till well blended.
- Put in piping bag. Fill inside of cupcakes.

Marshmallow Fluff:

- In electric mixer on high, beat egg whites and vanilla till stiff peaks form.
- In small pan over medium-high heat, combine sugar, crème of tartar, and water. Bring to boil.
- Slowly drizzle down side of mixing bowl into whipped egg mixture till completely blended.
- Put in piping bag and frost a flat circle on top of pie for emoji sugar rice paper faces.

Garnish and Topper:

- Cut out emoji faces from rice sugar paper and stick on top of marshmallow frosting.
- Or peel two emoji stickers at a time and place back to back around the tip of toothpick.

CHAPTER 6

SOBRIETY SHAKES

For my first experience on a yoga mat, I almost fainted and threw up. If you know anything about athletes, that is part of our training. If you're not puking at the end of a race, you left something out on the course. I was one of those athletes. Yes, the first time I went into a yoga class, with my *perfect* new outfit and mat, I spent most of the time in child's pose. The one who would not stoop so low as to put my running shoes on and not do at least five miles was unfit for a simple thing like yoga practice. So my first try at yoga did not disappoint. I felt like I was playing twister on steroids. I did not understand what the instructor was saying. So I would watch my neighbor on her mat and try to do what she did. I spent most of the time feeling like a failure. I had to push through the pain. No pain, no gain, right? Only in yoga it is supposed to be "no pain, no pain." I think that being humbled is a gift most overlooked by athletes. So I did what all perfection-seeking athletes do … I went back for more.

I went two to three times a week. I slowly improved. I was eventually able to stand on one foot in a pose or two. I experimented with hot yoga, Kundalini, and Ashtanga. All by accident. I did not really know there was a difference. I just went to a fitness gym that offered yoga. I went to whatever class was offered that fit my schedule. I even ended up in an inversion class. That almost ended my yoga career for good. Even a torn deltoid muscle could not defeat this athlete striving for perfection. I had a distorted view of what yoga was supposed to be like.

Fast-forward one year … I got certified in chair yoga from my sweet Lakshmi Voelker (Get Fit Where You Sit 2010). I know that seems like a leap. But if you are an athlete, you probably get this fast and furious path. The *Big Book of AA* talks about some people getting it quickly (Smith and Wilson 2001, 84). That was me. Although, I think they were talking about sobriety. I plunged in and never looked back. What I discovered in chair yoga is that it fit perfectly into my profession as a recreation therapist. You adapt the poses to meet the needs of people with *all* ability levels.

So I launched a research project and looked at the effects of chair yoga for persons with Alzheimer's disease (Litchke and Hodges 2014; Litchke, Hodges, and Reardon 2012). As I was leading the yoga and practicing it with the residents, I began to notice how the poses felt in my own body. I later learned a term in Sanskrit called *svadhyaya* or self-study, one of the Niyamas. I was trying on the chair poses and seeing how they fit in my body. I was sharing this experience with them. Then something incredibly unexpected happened right there in those assisted-living homes with my favorite people. In the middle of the morning, amidst the nurses dispensing medications, staff talking, kitchen staff preparing for lunch, and some residents pacing, I experienced my seventh miracle. A small wink from God. He showed up. I knew beyond a shadow of a doubt I was doing exactly what He wanted me to be doing. I had found God's purpose for my life ... sharing yoga with persons in need. This gift of yoga was a way to reach people with Alzheimer's by connecting with them spirit to spirit. One soul to another. This was God's thin place for me. Where I felt awe-inspired.

I feel closer to God's presence sharing yoga with these residents than anywhere else on earth. I feel like I am home. One of the residents greeted me one day saying, "Welcome home!" And that is exactly how I feel every time I go there. She was actually born on the same day as I was fifty years prior. And I get a funny feeling that she is going to be one of the first people I meet in heaven. The yoga research had such a positive impact that I continue to do yoga with them once a month. And every time, I get the same feeling; I am one with them and God. In the "now" moment of yoga. I am utilizing this beautiful gift of yoga that God gave me.

The first time my eighty-two-year-old dad came with me to watch the yoga, he wept. For years, he had no idea what I did as a recreation therapist. I always end our yoga practice with relaxation and singing "Amazing Grace." Residents' eyes will open up. They will start singing. My dad's eyes filled with tears. He finally got what a recreation therapist does. What I did. Just the other day, he told me I was a "prize." I cried. My cup runneth over. I just love my daddy. After our relaxation, it has become our tradition to do the chicken dance. That's how we celebrate souls coming together through yoga in central Texas!

As the fifth-year anniversary of my chair yoga certification approached, I decided to pursue my two-hundred-hour integrative yoga therapy teacher training in Hawaii from the Soma Institute for three weeks (Le Page 2007). I know what you are thinking. Had to be in Hawaii, right? Little did I know what other miracles were waiting for me on the Big Island. The two teachers, Liz and Molly, were amazing. The first day, we were told to pour out our teacups filled with yoga knowledge. That way there would be room enough for them to pour in the new yoga information. I liked that metaphor. So I dumped my cup.

The first week was so mentally and physically stressful. Five hours of yoga daily was just like the old days when I was training for triathlon competitions. So I relapsed back into the athlete mind-set. I was mentally challenging myself to overcome the physical challenges my body was experiencing. I felt like I was climbing a mountain and could not see the peak. Pulling and pushing my way to the top into those poses. I was homesick too. Off the grid and missing my family. We had homework every night. I felt so vulnerable. Alone. Then the strangest thing started to happen to me that had never happened in triathlon training. I found myself lying in bed at night chanting myself to sleep. More like singing off-key in Sanskrit. Not even sure I had the right words or pronunciations. But you get my drift. I even dreamt in Sanskrit. Something weird was happening here …

After week one, I reached the summit. I could see the beautiful view on the other side. And I liked what I saw. As I descended into Ayurveda work, I learned that my Dosha was Vata. And surprise, surprise, I was out of balance. Too much time spent in the air and ether. You see, I had developed irritable bowel syndrome (IBS) during my second year of sobriety. When I looked back at my journals, a pattern emerged. Every day at five, my stomach would hurt. Do you think that was a coincidence that every day at five I used to drink? I don't think so. The doctor said that for years I had been self-medicating my fears and anxiety with alcohol. I had also developed a public speaking, social anxiety disorder. Take away the alcohol, and my body and mind needed new coping mechanisms. I was all shook up. I took the doctor's advice and got on antidepressant medication to help manage my anxiety, all be it after much protest.

I hate to admit it, but it works. What the doctor explained to me was that the medication was just a piece of the bigger picture for wellness. The big hook came when he said, "You just won't have to work so hard to be calm. The medicine will just make things easier for you." I had to really wrap my mind around that to accept taking medication as not being a weakness. The question that kept going through my mind was, "With yoga, God, and sobriety, shouldn't I be strong enough not to need medication?" But what dawns on me every time I taper off the meds, (when I play MD instead of PhD), to see if I really need them or not, is that it is *not about me*. As an alcoholic, I am very aware that I think everything is all about me. Taking meds is not about just me. I am a better teacher, therapist, mom, wife, and friend when taking my medication. So it is about the others I am here to serve for God. So get over yourself, Lyn. Medication is just one of the pieces of the puzzle you are putting together to live in God's will. Also, my stomach is definitely not as bad. I can talk without a panic attack in front of my colleagues or giving student lectures. I can teach yoga with a sense of humor. I also started a special diet for my IBS called FODMAP. Coincidently, it is just like the Ayurveda-recommended Vata nutritional system. More dots connecting.

Being an out of balance Vata meant I needed to get back to earth and water. I took my shoes off. I began to reconnect to the earth by walking barefoot. Taking baths instead of showers. I began eating wet, dense food recommended for Vatas. I am not sure that strawberry lemonade *sobriety shake cupcakes* are part of that diet. But I can make them gluten-free, and that is on the diet.

My arrival in this place coincides with figuring out where God was taking me—and going there.

Strawberry Lemonade Sobriety Shake Cupcakes

(*Gluten-free; makes 30 cupcakes)

Cupcake Ingredients:
Popover baking pan
silver cupcake papers
3 cups gluten-free flour
1/2 teaspoon baking powder
1 teaspoon baking soda
1/2 teaspoon salt
2 sticks unsalted butter (softened)
2 cups granulated sugar
3 large eggs (room temperature)
2 teaspoons lemon peel grated (2 lemons)
1 teaspoon vanilla bean paste
2 cups sour cream (room temperature)

Filling:
1 cup heavy whipping cream
1/4 cup powder sugar
1 teaspoon vanilla bean paste
1 pint fresh strawberries

Frosting:
1 cup powder sugar
2 tablespoon heavy whipping cream
1 teaspoon fresh lemon juice
2 teaspoons strawberry icing fruit

Topper:
30 colorful bendy straws
30 colorful straw toppers
30 patterned scrap book patterned paper cut to look like soda cup
hot glue gun or clear tape
1 pint fresh strawberries

Directions:

- Preheat oven to 325 degrees F. Line popover pan with silver cupcake papers.
- In medium bowl, combine flour, baking powder, baking soda, and salt. Set aside.
- In electric mixer, combine butter and sugar till fluffy. Beat in eggs one at a time.
- Add lemon peel and vanilla bean paste.
- Lower mixer speed to lowest setting. Alternating between sour cream and dry ingredients in two portions, slowly add to mixer.
- Mix only till all ingredients are incorporated. Do not overmix.
- Bake for 25–30 minutes and cool completely.

Filling:

- In electric mixer whip heavy cream till soft peaks form.
- Add powder sugar and vanilla bean paste till stiff peaks.
- Mash strawberries in blender and fold into whip cream.
- Place in piping bag with large floret tip.
- Fill center of cupcakes.

Frosting:

- In small bowl, mix powder sugar, heavy whipping cream, lemon juice, and strawberry icing fruit.
- Dip top of cupcake in mixture.

Garnish and Topper:

- Cut colored patterned paper into 7 inches by 2 inches curved shape.
- Glue or tape to outside silver cupcake paper, leaving part of silver exposed at top.
- Cut straws in half.
- Slide straw tags over the bendy part of straw.
- Cut out small sayings and glue on top of straw sliders.
- Stick in center of cupcake into filling.
- Cut remaining strawberries in half.
- Garnish with dollop of filling and top with fresh strawberry.

*(design idea inspired by Tack and Richardson 2012).

CHAPTER 7

WALK BY FAITH

I found God in yoga. He was waiting right there for me in my old habits. I continued to struggle in my poses, trying to get my body to do what the person on the mat next to me was doing. I was vigilant in looking outside of myself at others. And I did not like what I saw. I was in a state of constant comparison. I was back to being an athlete and competing not only with everyone else in class but myself too. It got to the point where my skin actually began to hurt. The negative energy I was creating was causing me to suffer. Not to mention what that was doing to anyone else in the class. There is a term I learned in Hawaii during my yoga certification called *kleshas* or causes of suffering. Well, guess what one of the kleshas is? Ego! I realized it was my *ego* physically hurting my skin. And there I was edging God *o*ut again.

I was pretty hopeless at getting past the physicality of yoga. So how was I going to get unstuck from my physical body and gain access to the true essence of yoga underneath? The answer was in the *koshas*, described like layers of an onion. The five koshas begin on the outside with what we can see. Then peel away layer by layer to reveal the subtle innermost core of our being. What we cannot see. The first outermost layer is the physical body (Annamayakosha), which includes the poses and Ayurveda; the second layer underneath is the energy body (Pranamayakosha) involving our breath and chakras; the third layer represents our emotional body (Manomayakosha), including our thoughts, habits, and behaviors; followed by the fourth, wisdom body (Vijnayanamayakosha), involving our intellectual being as a self-witness; and finally revealing the core of the onion, our bliss body (Anandaamayakosha) or true identity. Where peace, joy, freedom, and connectedness with God reside (Le Page 2007).

I want to give you an example of how I actually came to know the koshas. It just so happened that during my Hawaiian training, one of my teachers, Liz, saw me struggling to get into my not so perfect, *perfect* physical body. Like trying on an outfit that was too tight and didn't fit. But I wanted so desperately for it to look good on me. As I frantically tried to squeeze my body into a difficult pose, my teacher gently brushed my shoulder, just with two fingers. She handed me a yoga block and said, "Just 60 percent effort, Lyn. Use your resources to support you." From then on, whenever she would touch me with her two fingers, I would be gently reminded to try on a different outfit.

I was 110 percent athlete. Not a 60 percent yogini. Like it or not, I needed to take it down a few notches. I thought using props was cheating or for those who were not good enough to master the pose. She invited me to operate differently. To think differently. To try on a different outfit that I never thought would look good on me. For a professor and straight-A student, I had to perform at a D level. That was a huge challenge for me. But what a precious gift she gave me! I put that knowledge in my teacup. I had to take a step outside myself and be my own witness. Watch myself in a pose. Be the pose. Not *do* the pose. She had shown me a way to embrace one of the subtler koshas, the wisdom body. The only way for me to embrace that was to be at 60 percent effort.

What I found at 60 percent effort was this space to grow into. In that space, there was this exquisite silence. That's where the secret lies. A 110 percent-er like me can feel the beauty of living at 60 percent effort. At 60 percent, I can quiet myself enough to tune in and listen to what my body and mind feel. I don't think alcoholics like to function at 60 percent. Because then we can hear what we don't want to hear. We have a problem. There is only one solution: "admit we are powerless over alcohol and turn our will and our lives over to God" (Smith and Wilson 2001, 59). I don't know what I expected, but it wasn't this. At the center of my onion, in the silence … was God.

I had finally created a space to accept myself without judgment. I surrounded myself and my mat with a judgment-free zone. I think God just wants us to create a space during yoga to invite Him in. In that not so perfect moment. Just as we are. Perfectly broken. Listening for Him to speak to us. He will. I know. Because He spoke to me.

When I got to my onion core, I began to rely on my faith. Faith in what I was feeling during each pose. Applying what I was learning during my teacher training and my newfound faith in God. I needed to *walk by faith*. Do yoga by faith. Take yoga off the mat into my life. Into the unknown. Embrace what I could not see. Like Martin Luther King said, "Faith is taking the first step without seeing the entire staircase." The stairs on this staircase were the layers of my onion. I was walking not only toward God but freedom. I had arrived at the fifth kosha, full of peace, joy. Free at last! Dr. King sure knew what he was talking about.

I think about all those years of my life I spent chained to fear. I was chained to worry, chaos, addiction, and my old friend perfection. I had come to realize that I was truly afraid to be free. How does that work? How do you live free? Because if I live free, then I would be in this totally unknown territory. I would have to look, act, and think differently on all levels. I would have to become unattached to my physical outer layer and live unstuck. No more chains. Nothing holding me back anymore. The kosha framework of yoga led me closer to God. And lo and behold, He came closer to me. Like two ends of a magnet unable to resist the attraction. I was *overcoming the sticky situation of addition*—not only to alcohol but my "Maya" or "illusion" of what and who I thought I was.

This illusion was revealed during my third Yoga Nidra experience in my certification training. Yoga Nidra is a form of deep sleep that combines relaxation, breath, affirmations, and visualizations. It is a profound meditative, hypnotic state. I had practiced Yoga Nidra twice before with much doubt and skepticism. But third time's the charm, right? It would become the first time I have ever heard the voice of God. Speaking to little ole me. Miracle number eight. Since then He has spoken to me a second time. More on that later.

The yoga room was light and airy that afternoon. A trade wind blowing across my skin. Eyes dreamily closed. Drifting in and out with each breath. When clear as a bell from the back, right side of my head, I heard God's voice whisper, "Lyn, go and tell them about me." I sat bolt upright. Opened my eyes. Looked around to see who was talking to me. Everyone else in the class was laying down on their mat, eyes closed. My teacher, Molly, who was guiding us just looked at me and smiled. I lay back down. All I could think about was Moses. Moses had a speech impairment. He told God he could not be His spokesperson or leader of His people. So if Moses had doubts, how was I going to tell people about God? After all, I had a public speaking anxiety disorder. I don't know what I expected. But it wasn't this.

I found myself thinking, *God deserves someone better than me. Someone cleverer. Someone with more faith. Someone like Dr. King, Gandhi. Or Mother Theresa. Not Lyn Litchke. But He chose me. So it's not up to me anymore. Or about me anymore.* That was the illusion, my Maya. It had been shattered during my Yoga Nidra experience. Sometimes God's voice is nothing more than a whisper, but you have to get quiet enough to listen. The koshas led me there. In the silence at 60 percent effort, in the new space between my breaths, in my newfound sobriety, there I was walking hand in hand with Jesus. I was found. Or He found me.

Journal sketch, "Walking Hand in Hand with Jesus."

God never fails to show up and give me something that is always way better or different from what I could ever ask for or imagine. Ephesians 3:20 is alive and well today. "Now all glory to God, who is able, through his mighty power at work within us, to accomplish infinitely more than we might ask or think." With cupcakes for dessert of course. After all, dessert spelled backwards is "stressed." We don't need more stress. So I took all those skills and thoughts I had perfected doing something to poison my body, mind, and spirit (drinking), and instead honoring my body, mind, and spirit through yoga. I put my yoga practice to work on faith. Walking by faith one *high-heel shoe* at a time.

By the way, one interpretation of Yoga Nidra is "Full of God." I am. He can have all of me.

Walk by Faith High-Heel Shoe Cupcakes

(Makes 30 cupcakes)

Cupcake Ingredients:
2 3/4 cups all-purpose soft wheat flour
2 teaspoons baking powder
1/2 teaspoon salt
1 stick unsalted butter, softened
1 cup high-ratio shortening
2 cups granulated sugar
4 large eggs
1 cup buttermilk
1 teaspoon almond extract
1 teaspoon vanilla extract

Filling:
1 (8-ounce) can of raspberry pastry filling
Or
2 pints raspberries
1/2 cup sugar
2 tablespoons fresh lemon juice
1/2 teaspoon cornstarch

Frosting:
2 sticks unsalted butter, softened
1 cup heavy whipping cream
1 teaspoon almond extract
1/4 teaspoon salt
16 ounces powdered sugar

Garnish:
1 can pirouette vanilla cookies
16 graham crackers
8 ounces vanilla or strawberry chocolate easy-melt candy
parchment paper
colored tube decorative frostings
edible pearls
edible glitter

Directions:
- Preheat oven to 325 degrees F. Line cupcake tins with color-stay decorative papers.
- Spray cupcake liners with vegetable spray.
- In medium bowl, sift flour, baking powder, and salt.
- In electric mixer, beat butter and shortening at medium speed till creamy.
- Gradually add sugar.
- Add one egg at a time. Mix after each egg.
- Put mixer on lowest speed and alternate between adding flour and buttermilk in two turns.
- Add extracts and mix till blended.
- Bake for 12–15 minutes or till toothpick comes out clean. Cool completely.

Filling:
- Combine raspberries, sugar, lemon juice, and cornstarch in medium sauce pan and stir to combine.
- Simmer for 10 minutes over medium-low heat, stirring occasionally.
- Cook till thickened and remove from heat. Cool for 15 minutes.
- Or use canned raspberry pastry filling.
- Scoop into piping bag with small tip.
- Fill center of cupcakes with raspberry filling.

Frosting:
- In electric mixer, whip butter and heavy whipping cream. Mix in extract.
- On lowest speed, add powder sugar and salt.
- Put in piping bag and frost cupcakes.
- Smooth frosting with a knife, leaving a small dome to form top of shoe.

Creating high-heel shoes:
- Cut pirouette cookies on an angle about 1 1/2 to 2 inches for the heels.
- Break graham crackers into marked rectangles and then use serrated knife and cut into flat, pointed triangle pieces.
- Heat chocolate easy-melt candy in microwave (about one minute on high).
- Spread melted chocolate on graham cracker and set on parchment paper till dry.
- Cut small half-moon shape out of the top of one side of frosted cupcake.
- On an angle, wedge larger flat end of chocolate-covered graham cracker into cutout portion of cupcake.

- Dip cut angle of pirouette cookie end into melted chocolate and adhere underneath the flat narrower end of graham cracker to form heel. Prop and let dry completely.
- Decorate top and heel of shoes to accentuate cupcake liner pattern.

*(design idea inspired by Tack and Richardson 2012).

CHAPTER 8

OUT OF THE DARK
INTO THE LIGHT

When we started chakra and meditation training, it was like this weird déjà vu thing. Like I had experienced this before. Which made me hesitate only for a moment. Then I jumped right in. It was the chakras that first got my full attention. Chakras are the life-force energy centers within the body. There are seven chakras representing separate energy channels connecting the nervous system and endocrine glands (Le Page 2007). I had tried Reiki (a healing technique of touch connecting to an individual's life-force energy) six months prior to coming to yoga training in Hawaii, to help my IBS. I drew a visual picture of my chakras from that Reiki session. Six months later, during my training in Hawaii, I drew them again. I included both drawings so you can see the transformation.

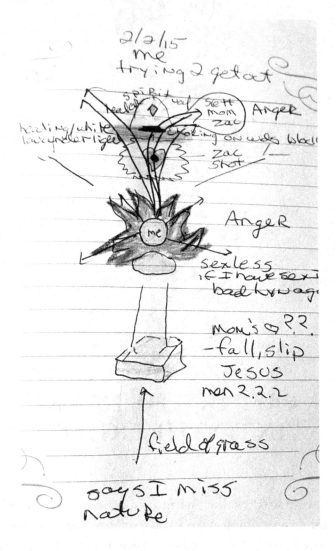

Journal sketch, "Chakra Reiki Drawing February 2015."

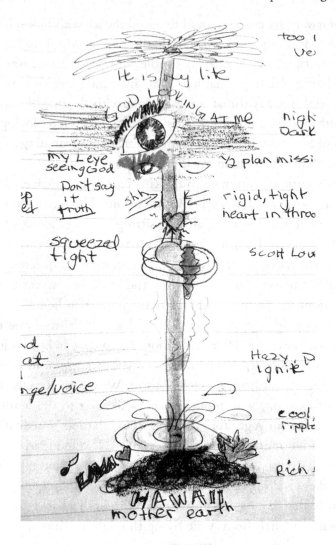

Journal sketch, "Chakra Hawaii Drawing July 2015."

The first drawing of my seven chakras revealed that I was standing on a block of ice, waiting to slip and fall. My second chakra was like the Sahara Desert. My third chakra was engulfed in rage and flames (my IBS). My heart chakra had a bullet hole in it. My throat chakra was like I was being choked … so blocked were my words. My third eye was just beginning to see the light. And my seventh chakra was just starting to bloom.

Fast-forward six months, and I replaced the ice with rich volcanic soil (Big Island love). My second chakra had a bloom. My third chakra had only a small flame like a birthday candle. My heart chakra was healing, and only half is bleeding. That half is my husband's love and my struggle with his drinking. My throat was still tight with the inability to tell the whole truth (more on this in the next chapter). I see God's loving eye but only half of His plan. I have too many visions. I am searching so hard for what God wants me to do in my life.

It was a curiously intimate thing, this chakra experience. Getting to feel and see what was transpiring inside of me. The meditation was not too different. I am pretty hopeless at sitting still. Let alone sitting still saturated in silence. Each morning of our training, our teacher exposed us to different styles of meditation. Concentrating on different types of breathing techniques. Using a mantra and mala beads. Various mudra hand positions. All in an attempt to "make yourself at home."

Each morning at six, my alarm would go off. It would be the only sound I would hear until after meditation. I would lay in bed for just a few moments, with my eyes closed, before venturing out into the cabin to see my roommates silently brushing their teeth. We were instructed to honor the start of each day with total silence. Walk over to the outdoor yoga pavilion. Gather our yoga props to prepare our "chariots" (meditation seat). After my initial squirming to find my chariot, I would grasp some mala beads, take a deep breath, and dive right in. Only to find my chattering mind monkeys waiting right there to greet me. Reminding me of things I needed to do that day. Asking me if I heard this or that background sound. All the while my mala beads were flying through my fingers.

We sat in silence for thirty minutes. I have never in my life sat still anywhere for thirty minutes. I was all over the place. I had to figure out how to sit without scratching an itch. Should I even use these mala beads? How many beads should I count each morning on my mala strand? As if you were even supposed to be counting them. Not. Which style of breath should I focus on? What should my intention or mantra be? My first *sankalpa* or intention in meditation was "I am doing God's plan for my life." Which my teacher interpreted as close as she could in Sanskrit to "Om Prasada Namah" or "I bow to grace." I added God. So I started there. I would slide in and out of my meditative space repeating my mantra one bead at a time. Using one breath cycle, per bead, per mantra. A thought would poke its way in, and I would say hello and send it on its way back out to the universe.

I improved over time. Even if it was only to find a better way to sit upon my chariot. Miracle number nine showed itself to me in the class called Introduction to Walking Meditation. The truth of the matter was that I was convinced walking meditation was not going to be for me. I had just learned to sit still for goodness sake. Now you want me to walk and meditate at the same time? That's not going to happen. But there was no way around it. When I took the very first step, something was different. Below is the excerpt from my journal in Hawaii 7/28/15:

> First day of walking mediation, I did not just get a wink from God, but He actually showed me a vision. What He wanted me to see. Now that was a huge unexpected miracle. I knew immediately when I took that first step I was not going to leave the room. Our teacher had told us to start walking in the room for the first five minutes, then walk to the beach. I was saying my sankalpa, "Om Prasada Namah," with each part of my foot. On "Om," I pressed my heel down; then on "Prasada" the soul of the foot; and finally, my toes touched the floor on "Namah." Slowly, softly, and carefully, I stepped as everyone left the room but me and one of my favorite classmates. Then I froze. I saw this emanating radiant light on the floor in front of me and the darkness behind me. I was coming out of the darkness and into the light. I had my hands crossed at the wrist behind my back as I walked. I stopped dead in my tracks. One tear rolled down my cheek. I was warped back to the time when my son was handcuffed and taken away from me to jail. To the time when wine had my hands chained behind my back. I was walking in meditation, and God showed me I was on the right path. These steps of faith had led me right to this exact moment to see and feel that I was not afraid to be free.

After class, the teachers asked for feedback on our first walking meditation experience. I was so uncomfortable. Not sure I could even speak. Most of the students did not have much to say. But I knew even with my public speaking anxiety, I really needed to do this. Tell them what happened to me. I raised my hand. I was trembling. My words rang out in the still air. "I am in a twelve-step recovery program. Those steps became very real for me in this room. I just celebrated my third year of sobriety here in Hawaii. And the power of the light before me, dark shadow on the floor behind me, and the handcuffs were so surreal. I know now I am on the right path." I cried then. Not sobbing. The tears left me silently and told me something else had left me. Shame. Guilt. Fear. What a relief to speak and not hide this secret of being an alcoholic anymore. Nobody had ever heard me say those words aloud before. I had just outed myself in public for the very first time.

Later that night, I was going to get my third-year sobriety chip and be the speaker at an AA meeting during my stay in Hawaii. In preparation, I was thinking about what God had whispered to me during my Yoga Nidra experience, about telling people about Him. After all, He is the reason I am sober today. And I recalled how God had recruited Moses. So that night, I brought my *Life Recovery Bible* with me to AA. I shared it with the group. I told them about the God of my understanding, Jesus. And how he saved my life. I told them about yoga. And how I found God there. I even demonstrated a few yoga poses. The "happy hour" pose or legs up the wall. And one of Pa Taun Chin Eight Essential Seated Exercises called "clenching the fist with attentive eyes," which reduces anger and toxins from your liver. It was one of the best talks of my life as a sober Christian! Afterwards, a woman came up to me and told me she was going to buy that book.

Then it dawned on me. What if everything I do or say is about God? Let my words, be His words. Even if the words I use are in Sanskrit, or on my cupcakes, or bumper stickers. Let my actions be His. Let people look at me or my car and wonder what it is about me that is different, strange, weird, enlightening, joyful, contagious. It's Jesus living and working in all aspects of my life.

Wow, I am getting a funny feeling (déjà vu). I am on to something pretty spectacular!

Out of the Dark Chocolate into the White Light Cones

(Makes 24 cupcake cones)

Cupcake Ingredients
24 flat-bottom ice-cream cones
push-pop cake pan

Chocolate Batter:
4 ounces dark chocolate

Batter:
1 1/2 cup cake flour (sifted)
1 teaspoon baking powder
1 teaspoon baking soda
1/8 teaspoon salt
1 1/2 sticks unsalted butter (room temperature)
1 1/4 cups sugar
3 large eggs (room temperature)
1 teaspoon vanilla extract
1/3 cup buttermilk (room temperature)

Vanilla Batter:
1 1/2 teaspoons lemon peel (1 lemon)

Buttercream Frostings:
Optional striper pastry bag
1/2 cup heavy whipping cream
2 sticks unsalted butter (room temperature)
8 ounces softened cream cheese
1 1/2 teaspoons vanilla extract
1 pinch salt
1 1/2 cups powder sugar

Chocolate Frosting:
1/3 cup dark chocolate coco powder

Garnish and Toppers:
12 precut saying "Out of dark chocolate into white light"
12 small wooden ice-cream spoons
4 ounces dark chocolate candy melts or bark
1/2 pint of strawberries
Jimmy sprinkles

Directions:
- Preheat oven to 350 degrees F. Place oven rack in the middle position.
- Place cones in push-pop pan.
- Melt dark chocolate in microwave-safe bowl (30–60 seconds). Set aside.
- In medium bowl, combine cake flour, baking powder, baking soda, and salt.
- In electric mixer, combine butter and sugar. Add one egg at a time. Add vanilla. Mix on medium high till fluffy.
- Lower mixer speed to lowest setting. Alternating between buttermilk and dry ingredients in two portions, slowly add to mixer.
- Take half the batter out and place in medium bowl. Add lemon peel to the bowl and mix till just incorporated.
- Add melted chocolate to batter left in mixer.
- Mix only till all ingredients are incorporated. Do not overmix.
- Place vanilla and chocolate batters into separate 12-inch piping bags. Place them side by side in a larger 18–24-inch piping bag. Cut the end of all three bags.
- Squeeze both batters by twirling the mixture into bottom of cones till it comes all the way to the top.
- Bake for 15 minutes or till toothpick comes out clean. Cool completely.

Buttercream Frostings:
- In electric mixer, whip heavy whipping cream till soft peaks form. Scoop out and set aside.
- In same mixer on high, beat butter, cream cheese, vanilla, and salt till smooth and silky.
- Lower mixer to lowest setting and slowly add powder sugar.
- Fold in whipped cream.
- Scoop half the frosting into 12-inch piping bag. Or use striper pastry bag.
- Add coco powder to remaining frosting and beat till smooth.
- Place chocolate frosting into 12-inch piping bag.
- In large 18-inch piping bag, add decorative tip.
- Cut tips off bottom of both frostings and slide side by side into larger piping bag.
- Frost cupcake with a twirl like an ice-cream cone.

Garnish and Topper:

- Melt dark chocolate melts/bark in microwave on high for 1 minute. Stir.
- Dip half of the wooden ice-cream spoon in chocolate. Let dry on parchment paper.
- Hot glue the precut sayings to wood portion of spoon not dipped in chocolate.
- Stick into frosting. Top with chopped strawberries and Jimmy sprinkles.

CHAPTER 9

EVERYTHING IS BETTER
WITH BACON

B e careful what you say and do in yoga because your true inner feelings are going to be revealed. Those bottled-up, swallowed-up feelings are coming out. Especially if you go upside down. Part of my yoga training was inversions and backbends. I went to Hawaii, saying to myself, "I am not going upside down." I certainly did not think at my age I could do a backbend or stand on my head. I was too scared that I would break my neck. Well, with a wall, blocks, or a chair for support, I can do both. This type of practice helps open your heart chakra, "Anahata," and throat chakra, "Vsihuddha." I am giving you fair warning that working on improving yourself this way is not always easy.

Part of the inversion process is seeing things from a different perspective (literally upside down). And finding answers to life's questions you didn't even know to ask. Wheel pose decreases your shame. You are so vulnerable in that position with all your chakras open. Shoulder stand comes with great responsibility of supporting and trusting in yourself and the process. Going upside down is the most potent change in energy in your body. It can even reduce gray hair. I am in! It is no wonder that I can no longer remain quiet. My body, mind, and spirit won't let me. My chakra drawings say it all. My mind and body are communicating to my soul what I need. That's for sure. My second chakra drawing in Hawaii during my yoga therapy certification was surefooted in lava. But my heart and throat were damaged. If you look at what I wrote, it says, "Scott's (my husband) love melting away from my heart. Squeezed tight." Next to my throat, I wrote, "Rigid, tight, heart in throat, pressure. Don't say it. Truth. Keep quiet."

What did not dawn on me with these chakra drawings is that there is always another drawing to follow. You will always continue to evolve and change if you keep practicing yoga. In yoga they call that *sachitananda*. So there I was at home for two months after my healing Hawaii trip, my IBS dormant, and now my throat physically hurt. I kept going upside down. And I saw what had been strangling me. And no, I don't want to talk about it! But what I know to be true is that I self-selected those poses for my home individual yoga practice. I deep down wanted to open the fourth and fifth chakras. I am in need of telling the truth. So out it comes. I am seeing a truth I do not want to see. I am finding a voice that is causing my husband and me so much pain. My throat actually hurts daily. I burp and feel the pressure of indigestion. I just want to feel better.

Yoga Sutras by Pantanjali taught me about the *yamas* and *niyamas* (Bachman 2011). They remind me of the Ten Commandments in the Bible. Two of the yamas are called "sayata" and "ahimsa" or truthfulness and non-harm, respectively. So this not telling the truth is harming me and making me sick. So here is my truth … I just never know when my husband, Scott, comes home at night who is walking through the door. Is it the real him or drinking him? Why do I see such a difference? I just don't know who I am dealing with. I get nervous, scared, and anxious. Do I ask him or say something so I know? And if I do that, isn't that so messed up? It is like living with my mom all over again. Living in uncertainty with someone I love trips my trauma triggers that are carved so deep in my brain. I work to create a new neuropathway in my brain through counseling, praying, yoga, going to church, cupcakes, and more, and then I slide back into that deep trauma groove in my brain. I am back on the ice. But one thing about yoga, it won't allow me to push it down inside anymore. Or should I say the true essence of Lyn won't let me push it down inside anymore. I want to heal. Only I keep falling back into this ditch. Is this the ditch my son was in when he was doing drugs? To avoid pain? In the ditch I go. In he went. Only this time I won't use wine. "Devil, you can't have me back!" I feel God's armor protecting me. I feel those angels surrounding me on all sides. The devil is taking my health and my husband. And I am letting him.

Why should I even need to ask if he has been drinking? I need to get off the ice and back to barefoot in the lava. Why does it matter so much to me that he gets sober? We have tried counseling. We keep coming back to this place where I do okay for a while but then start doing inversions, and out comes the truth. I talked to him again for the umpteenth time about how I feel. What I need. He tells me again. He is not ready to quit drinking. I know it is the craving of his physical body, not his spiritual body. But I secretly hope he gets pulled over by the police. So he hits bottom, and they make him go to AA and stop drinking. I even told him that. So I guess it is not a secret anymore. What if he gets hurt? What if he hurts someone else? I need to go to Al-Anon. I am so codependent.

I have been praying and asking God, where is my husband's bottom? When will he get there? I want to move forward. It has been three years. We are not good at communicating. We were both raised to not talk about issues. We have been like this for over twenty years. I married my best friend and drinking buddy. He is so loving, caring, sweet, and so funny when he is not drinking. For my birthday, he surprised me with these deliciously warm *meatloaf cupcakes with mashed potato frosting topped with bacon* (gluten-free of course). But I changed the rules of our marriage. Three years ago, I quit drinking and became a Christian. I knew I was rolling the dice on whether or not our marriage would survive. I don't see my life without him. I love him so much.

This is tiring. I need more counseling ... and a cupcake (with some protein for energy).

Meatloaf Mashed Potato and Bacon Cupcakes

(*Gluten-free; makes 6 large cupcakes)

Cupcake Ingredients:
Large cupcake pan
baking spray
3 pounds lean ground beef
1/2 cup milk
2 eggs

3/4 cup gluten-free bread crumbs
1 teaspoon coarse kosher salt
1/2 teaspoon pepper

Frosting:
3–4 medium potatoes
3 tablespoon butter
1/2 cup milk
1/4 teaspoon coarse kosher salt
1/8 teaspoon pepper

Garnish:
6 pieces of bacon (cooked and chopped)

Directions:
- Preheat oven to 350 degrees F. Spray inside of large cupcake pan.
- Hand mix meat, milk, eggs, bread crumbs, salt, and pepper in large bowl.
- Divide meatloaf mixture evenly between cupcake tins.
- Bake for one hour.
- Meanwhile, in pan on stovetop, cook up bacon till crispy. Set aside to cool. Then chop.

Frosting:
- Peel and chop potatoes and place in salted boiling water.
- Boil 10 minutes or until fork tender. Drain potatoes and place in electric mixer.
- In electric mixer with potatoes, add butter, milk, salt, and pepper.
- Whip on medium-high till fluffy.
- Put large tip in piping bag and add mashed potatoes.
- Take meatloaf cupcakes out of tin and then pipe with potatoes.

Garnish:
- Sprinkle bacon over top of cupcakes.

CHAPTER 10

CARROT CAKE FOR CHRIST

I have been seeing a new Christian counselor, Richard Laosa, on and off since moving to our dream home by the river. (Although I still keep in touch with Kelly.) He is an expert at combining neuroscience and spirituality. I like when science and devotion to God collide. He taught me the most fascinating thing about myself. Why this is so surprising I am not sure. But I found out that I am not just addicted to alcohol. I am addicted to this behavior pattern that I seem to have established a long time ago with my mom and now have carried that over with my spouse. In yoga, these patterns are called *samskaras* or imprints. Needless to say, these imprints can turn into addictions.

When I was young and nervous or scared, I would get a stomach ache. In my childhood, my mom would run upstairs yelling and crying, and I would be left not knowing what I did to cause her to be so mad or sad. So even today when I find myself scared, my stomach hurts. Hence, the IBS. You know what made me feel better? Oh this will so surprise you. Drinking wine! Of course, it relaxed me and temporarily eased the pain in my stomach. But ever since I quit using wine to calm my nerves, my stomach hurts.

I subsequently established a pattern with my spouse of not telling him the truth about his behavior bothering me. I never spoke to my mom about her behavior either. I was too afraid. So I started to swallow my emotions and feel indigestion. Like I was being choked. What a metaphor. Your body and mind are so connected. We use all these sayings like "pain in the neck" or "that makes me sick to my stomach." Well, I was truly experiencing those things. You add the yoga inversions and backbends, and my throat chakra could no longer contain my feelings. So here I was just circling back to this place of discomfort. That same place that somehow my body recognizes as a comfortable place to be. It is what I have always known. Not sure if that makes any sense or not. I am just so used to being and acting sick that my body craves this as normal. My body needs to get its "sick fix." Our lack of marital communication, in regards to our unhealthy lifestyle, has become our norm. My body seeks it to provide a state of homeostasis (balance). When my counselor explained that to me, it finally clicked in my brain. I get it. More so you get it too.

Richard asked me if I was finally ready to rid myself of this last addiction. God has brought me to the point of trust in Him that I can no longer tolerate living in addiction of any kind. Well, besides being addicted to God of course.

Richard described to me that my brain had coded all my cells and even my DNA with a sickness marker caused by this need to live in uncertainty with poor communication. I have repeated that code for fifty years in other areas of my life to the point of addiction. So now my brain dumps bad chemicals into my system every time I get these negative emotions tied to these uncertain feelings. These chemicals travel to all my cells, especially the ones in my digestive system. And then my poor cells get sick and tell my brain we are back to where we know to live, and find stability in an unstable chemical situation. Like the temporary relief you get with that first sip of alcohol, and the reward system in your brain kicks in and says, "Ah …" And then for an alcoholic like me, "I want more." But my faith in God and my yoga practice no longer allow me to find relief and balance doing this.

But now that I am here, I am finally ready to conquer my last addiction and recode my cells. I am going to replace the old habits, samskaras, with new ones, so my brain will now dump happy chemicals into my body instead of bad ones. I will now try living from a place of comfort by confronting my discomfort. I am doing this by learning to be open and honest with my spouse about his behavior. And how I am letting that affect my health. Here are some of my new habits: doing yoga, going to counseling, talking to family and friends, going to church, reading my Bible each morning, having coffee with Jesus, listening to Christian music in my car, baking cupcakes, and daily meditation and prayer. I am not much of a computer person, but I imagine it is like writing a new computer code for a program you want to run. My brain is the computer. My new happy, healthy habits are the codes. And the results are my new happy cells. I even drew one of my new happy cells. It is a sunshine yellow circle with a pretty pink center nucleus. It has a furry coating of soft hairs to help it gently float throughout my entire body. My cell is almost smiling. Makes me so happy to see it in my mind's eye and transfer it to paper, so I have a record of what my new, pretty healthy cell looks like.

10/6/15

My newly coded
Happy Healthy Joyful
Cells

My last addiction is
coming to an end.

Journal sketch, "Happy, Healthy Cell."

So I visualize that newly coded cell making its way down my throat to my stomach and intestines. Along the way bumping into all my other sick cells and recoding them with chemicals of joy. Now they all can be smiling cells. I am beginning to sense this final destination as a great place to rest and find a new homeostasis. I guess we all get used to what we know and are reluctant to change. We get scared of the unknown, so we stay stuck. Afraid to explore what God really has coded for our lives ... to reflect Him in all we say and do. I think I am finally ready to completely set myself free. I know that this only comes with support, and I have got that in place. I know carrots help your eyesight. I think I am ready to see the truth at last. To prepare myself, I think I'll go bake some *carrot cake for Christ*. Because if I know God, when I open my eyes, I am going to see another miracle, and I may need a snack. So here goes …

My husband made an appointment to see Richard.

Carrot Cake for Christ Cupcakes

(Makes 24 deconstructed cupcakes)

Cupcake Ingredients:
angel food cake pan
vegetable spray
baking sheet / parchment paper
extra-large decorative cupcake papers/liners
2 1/2 cups unbleached all-purpose flour (sifted)
1 teaspoon salt
1 teaspoon baking soda
2 teaspoons baking powder
1 1/2 teaspoons cinnamon
I pound grated carrots
3 large eggs (room temperature)
2 cups granulated sugar
1/3 cup buttermilk
1 1/2 cups vegetable oil
1 1/2 teaspoons vanilla extract
3/4 cup raisons (save 30 toppers)
1 cup pecans (toasted and chopped), divided
1/4 cup brown sugar

Frosting:
1/2 cup heavy whipping cream
12 ounces softened cream cheese
1/2 cup powder sugar
1/8 teaspoon salt
1 teaspoon vanilla

Garnish and Toppers:
1/2 cup pecans (toasted and chopped)
45 toothpicks
30 "Carrot Cake 4 Christ" sayings
30 raisons

Directions:
- Preheat oven to 325 degrees F. Spray angel food cake pan with vegetable oil. Line baking sheet with parchment paper.
- Sift flour, salt, baking soda, baking powder, and cinnamon in separate bowl.
- Grate carrots and set aside.
- In mixer, combine eggs, sugar, buttermilk, oil, and vanilla extract.
- Mix in raisons and carrots.
- Add dry ingredients and mix just till incorporated.
- Fold in 1/2 cup toasted pecans. Just till combined.
- Place 1/2 cup pecans in bottom of angel food cake pan and sprinkle with brown sugar.
- Pour cake mixture over nuts and sugar into angel food cake pan.
- Bake for 45 minutes. Remove from oven and turn out cake mix onto parchment-lined baking sheet. Separate with fork or knife into chunk-size pieces.
- Return to oven on 400 degrees F for 15 minutes. Gives it crunchy sweet deliciousness.
- Cool completely and separate chunks evenly into decorative extra-large cupcake liners.

Frosting:
- In electric mixer on high, whip heavy cream till it peaks. Scoop into small bowl. Set aside.
- In same mixer, beat cream cheese, powder sugar, salt, and vanilla on low speed till blended.
- Fold in whipped cream.
- Put in piping bag and dollop on deconstructed carrot cake.

Garnish and Topper:
- Cut fifteen toothpicks in half. Skewer raisons on whole toothpick and insert half toothpicks through raison so it looks like a cross.
- Cut out small sayings. Use glue gun to adhere to top of toothpick.
- Sprinkle with pecans.

CHAPTER 11

SLIDING ON

My husband has been seeing Richard for a few weeks, and things are remarkably better. Just a miracle itself that my spouse would go see a counselor on his own. Miracle number ten if you are keeping track. He is ready to begin his personal healing process. We have been very loving and caring toward each other as we move forward into our twentieth year of marriage. Last time I saw Richard, he asked me "Lyn, are you ready to heal? Is it your harvest time?" I answered a nail-biting "Yes!" I had no idea (as is usual with me and God) what would happen. God is so full of surprises.

Here's a surprise. Since January 1, 2011 (1/1/11), my baby sister, Ann Gorbett (aka Nina), told me about her gift of seeing the number 1 alongside other 1s. Nothing unusual unless you know how lucky my little sister is. She wins stuff, including money (bingo when we were little, $1,000). She sees stuff. Like a plane crash. On water. On a beach. That she happens to be at. With people walking off the plane unharmed. She takes pictures. And a newspaper buys the pictures from her for cash … I could go on. But the point is since she mentioned seeing 1s, I started noticing them too. I started looking for my number "1s." When I found them … they seemed bad luck at first. But I know different now. Zac's jail number "R*1*." I got saved by Jesus in 20*11*. I got sober at age 5*1* at an AA meeting at *11*:00 a.m. I see 1:11 p.m. and 11:11 a.m./p.m. all the time. It makes me smile. When I see those times on a clock, I think of my sisters, my mom, and Jesus. I am not alone (alone is the number 1). Get it?

Recently, when I see the time 1:11 or 11:11, I often take a picture of the clock and send it to my sisters. I also keep getting the feeling it has to do with my mom trying to tell me something. I began to get this image in my spiritual third eye during meditation of my mom standing in the distance alongside a paved path in lush green grass. Like she was standing there waiting for me to see her. Waiting to tell me something. She is in this certain dress that I recall her wearing at a party when she was so happy to be with me and my sons. One of the ways my mom showed me love was when she was with my boys. She just doted on them. Like she would have doted on me when I was little, if she had known how to back then. And then it happened, miracle number eleven (*11*). Surprise, surprise!

One of the best parts of my job is when I get to teach yoga to the university's women's golf team. I just love to watch them compete. So the last time I went to see them play golf, get ready … I saw the path in my vision. It was a golf cart path! And there was my mom! Now, I was not hallucinating, just seeing her with my celestial eyes versus the terrestrial eyes. (Those are the terms our counselor, Richard, uses to describe separating the spirit of a person from their physical body). Now my mom loved to play golf. We lived on a golf course for fifteen years. And there she was standing next to the path in that dress from my vision. She came over to me, and I could feel her love me. I was filled with joy and forgiveness. I wept … right there sitting on my golf stool next to the putting green on hole number … you guessed it—11. I knew in my heart of hearts that she would have loved to watch those girls golf with me. I treat the girls on the golf team like my daughters. And here was my mom treating me like her daughter. Like she was so proud of me. We shared a moment that I never had with her when she was alive.

Then it hit me ... what I needed to heal from. I always had this giant fear of walking on slippery ice about to fall when I was around her. Just like my first chakra drawing. It left me struggling with abandonment issues. My mom died so young at age sixty, just when we were starting to get close through her relationship with my sons. It was the final abandonment. She left me. She died. And on that golf course, that day, I realized she didn't abandon me in her death. She came back for me. She is there every time I see the *ones* together. We are united as *one*. Mother and daughter. I forgave her. It is my harvest time. Time to live forgiven. I even look different. Forgiveness has a look. I promise. Try it.

My younger sister has started a beautiful legacy in honor of our mother. She is an artist. You should go to her blog and commission a palette knife painting (Gorbett 2016). Anyway, when we were young, she used to make paper dolls and clothes from scratch. I know, pretty incredible talent, huh? We also used to play Barbie dolls together, and our mom would actually sew us doll clothes. So this past Christmas, she made doll clothes and bought dolls to look like me and our older sister, Cathy (aka Gina). She even gave each of us our alias names. I am *Luna*, Ann is *Nina*, and our Cathy is *Gina*. We love them. Best gift ever! So on our mom's birthday this year, my sisters and I spontaneously (without knowing each other was doing it) got our dolls dressed up in party clothes and began texting pictures of them to each other to celebrate. We had a birthday party for our mom with our dolls via text from Boston, to Texas, to Wyoming! Guess what time was on the clock when we were all texting during her cyber birthday party? You guessed it—11:11 p.m. I took a picture of the clock to commemorate that special day. The doll family has grown as my sisters and I made our mom's three sisters dolls of their very own. We each have one of our mom's original hand-sewn Barbie/Ken outfits that has been embellished in her honor. I even made a doll for my husband for our twentieth anniversary. Complete with homemade outfits. His alias is Shanti. By the way, that means peace.

I recently decided to *slide on* across the country and take my doll Luna and my latest cupcake, P&B and jelly sliders, on a road trip to write the last chapter of this book in honor of my newfound fearless freedom. I wanted my journey across the country to emulate the professional women who wrote the books *High-Functioning Alcoholics* (Benton 2010) and *Eat,*

Pray, Love (Gilbert 2010). Both about strong women's personal struggles, offering hope to readers about triumphing over alcohol or love. My plan was for a cross-country tour of America that would start with cupcake school at Make It Sweet in Austin, Texas (see appendix A for all the cupcake baking tips I learned), followed by a visit to Thorncrown Chapel in Eureka Springs, Arkansas, stopping by any roadside crosses I saw along the way, and finally to a yoga and recovery conference at Kripalu in Massachusetts where I would also assist my teacher Lakshmi in a chair yoga teacher training.

Road trip ... filled with cupcakes, yoga, and Jesus.

Peanut Butter and Jelly Slider Cupcakes

(Makes 18 cupcakes or 2 dozen mini cupcakes)

Cupcake Ingredients:
1 1/4 cups unbleached all-purpose flour
1/4 teaspoon salt
1 teaspoon baking soda
1 stick unsalted butter (softened)
3/4 cup crunchy peanut butter
3/4 cup brown sugar
2 extra-large eggs (room temperature)
1 teaspoon vanilla extract
1/4 cup milk (room temperature)

Strawberry Jelly Filling:
1 pint strawberries
1 cup sugar
1/2 teaspoon balsamic vinegar
4 tablespoons water, divided
1 teaspoon cornstarch

Peanut Butter Frosting:
1/2 cup heavy whipping cream
1 stick unsalted butter (softened)
12 ounces cream cheese (softened)
1 teaspoon vanilla extract
1 cup peanut butter
1 cup powder sugar

Toppers:
18–48 toothpicks
PB&J slider sayings

Directions:
- Preheat oven to 350 degrees F. Line cupcake tins with regular or mini color-stay papers.
- In medium bowl, combine flour, salt, and baking soda.
- In electric mixer, combine butter, peanut butter, and sugar. Add one egg at a time.
- Add vanilla. Mix on medium high till fluffy.
- Lower mixer speed to lowest setting. Alternating between milk and dry ingredients in two portions, slowly add to mixer.
- Mix only till all ingredients are incorporated. Do not overmix.
- Bake for 20 minutes or till toothpick comes out clean. Cool completely.
- Remove from cupcake paper. Cut cupcakes in half like a slider.

Strawberry Filling:
- Cut tops off strawberries and dice.
- On medium heat combine strawberries, sugar, balsamic vinegar, and 2 tablespoons water.
- Bring to boil. Reduce to medium-low.
- Cover and simmer 15 minutes.
- In small bowl, whisk cornstarch and 2 tablespoons water. Mix thoroughly.
- Add mixture to strawberries and stir constantly for 1–2 minutes till thickens.
- Remove from heat and cool.
- Put a tip in piping bag and fill with strawberry jelly.
- Place bottom half of cupcake bun in new cupcake liner and fill with strawberry jelly and top with other half of cupcake bun.

Frosting:
- In electric mixer on high, whip heavy cream till fluffy. Scoop into separate bowl and set aside.
- In same electric mixer on medium high, beat butter, cream cheese, and vanilla.
- Add peanut butter and powdered sugar on low and mix thoroughly.
- Fold in whipped cream just till well blended.
- Put in piping bag. Frost cupcakes.

Garnish and Topper:
- Cut out small sayings.
- Use glue gun to adhere to top of toothpick.

CHAPTER 12

ALL MY JOY

I do all my best thinking in my closet. I set up a prayer warrior room in my closet after seeing the movie *War Room* (2015). And that is where I go most mornings to meditate, pray, and go upside down. In the dark. There is something so spiritual about the darkness as I go in search of God's light. So there I was, in the dark, sitting upon my mediation chariot seat, in this sacred space, when it hit me that I needed to become a prayer warrior for my husband. Whatever happens, I need to let the devil know that he cannot have my husband. I write prayers for people on post-it notes and stick them on my warrior wall in the closet. Here's what I posted for my husband: *You can't have my husband back. He is sober and he is God's!* That was my personal shout out to the devil to get out of my house.

Because he was back.

This part of the story is not a happy one. My husband had quit going to see Richard, our counselor. Chapter 9 all over again. Will this sound strange that it was almost comforting? This feeling was familiar. Even though it was a bad feeling. I knew what it was. Codependency, I know only too well. And the search for booze was on. Not that Scott ever out and out hid it from me, but his behavior toward me changed dramatically. He withdrew from most contact with me physically and emotionally. Have you ever gone looking for something in earnest that you really didn't want to find? Such a strange feeling to have your feet taking you to a place you don't want to go. It was almost like my feet were leading me on their own accord. The exact same feeling I had walking my son to his sentencing. It was like my eyes were a video camera, and I needed to find the subject matter to document on film. And there in the video lens of my eyes, in the garage, in the trash can, just some innocent empty Coke cans. But my husband doesn't drink Coke unless there is bourbon. And on the movie screen playing out before my eyes was the almost-empty bottle of booze, tucked away, on the floor, by the fridge, in a brown crumpled bag.

I became the bag. I crumpled too, right there on my garage floor. I kept repeating aloud … "Oh no, oh no, oh no, oh noooooooooooooooooooooo oooooooo … not again."

What to do, what to do, what to do. Pray. Plead. Cry. Call my older sister. Cry some more. Repeat a phone call I made to her six months prior when I found the other empty bottle of booze in the trash. You probably know my next step … to make a deal. I upped my mandate post-it prayer note to the devil and began my campaign with God. And you all know how that usually turns out. I made a deal with God. I told God that if he wanted me to confront Scott *again*, that I would only agree to do so *if* (that's the big, capital IF) when he came home that night, 1) he acted like he had been drinking, 2) there was a cooler in his truck, and 3) he fell asleep right away.

He came home. He had been drinking. He fell asleep. It was time. I rose quietly out of bed to not disturb him. There were my feet walking me back to the garage and out to his truck. I said a prayer (or made a deal). "Dear, God, if there is an empty beer in the truck, then I will talk to him." It was like I was going in slow motion or swimming under water as I approached his truck. I was afraid he would awaken and find me. I opened the door to his truck as quietly as possible. And there on the front seat was the cooler with a towel covering over it. It was like an out-of-body experience. I lifted the towel and opened the lid. There were empty bottles of beer inside. I could not un-see what I saw or go back on my word to God. The strangest thing about this crisis was that I was ready to surrender. Wave the white flag. I was done. The battlefield of my mind and soul were surrendering the fight. I was at the finish line. I was ready to end my competition with alcohol. My war room hutzpah was gone.

I went to sit on the front porch to go through my THINK acronym and decide the words to say to him. Well, he awoke and came on the porch and asked what I was doing out there. And I asked if he had been drinking and driving that night. He answered in his *usual* way, "I only have one beer after I ride my bike on the way home." I replied, in the *usual* way, "That was not what I asked." I began to cry and said, "I want you to know that it has come down to you going to rehab or me leaving. I don't feel that you will get better unless I leave. I am leaving so you can get better. I need to find a place to live. I will not be a part of this unhealthy lifestyle any longer. I need to feel safe. I feel alone and unsafe."

I found myself giving him the ultimatum I know I am not supposed to give. Or ever thought I would be brave enough to do. I was just so tired of being brave. Exhausted really. True codependent behavior through and through. My trip was taking on a whole new meaning. I could feel him going away from me. But I had been leaving too. I was going to drive across the country alone. Not exactly the last chapter I thought I would be writing for this book, that's for sure. A different last chapter altogether.

The next day, he woke up and said he would go to rehab, but he was scared. He went to an AA meeting that night. Then the next night. Then he quit going. He called Richard and made an appointment. He went to meet with an outpatient rehab center. He told me that they did not want to talk about what he wanted to talk about, so he was not going to go back. I made an appointment to see Richard. I was so confused again. Richard told me, "From confusion comes clarity." That really hit home and stuck with me. So I made it into a new bumper sticker.

I decided to augment my trip itinerary and added all kinds of outdoor adventures, such as rock climbing, white-water rafting, camping, and zip-lining, to my original cupcake class, roadside crosses, and yoga school. I needed to do things I was afraid of because I needed to conquer my remaining fears. The biggest one, losing my husband. Who I am still so desperately in love with.

I think subconsciously I wanted Scott to come with me. I began telling him about the new wonderful outdoor adventures I had added to my trip. I tempted him. Dropped hints that he could come if he was sober. I wanted him to get sober so badly. I thought if he came with me and had so much fun getting "high" naturally, he would know he could quit. And if I am being honest, *choose me over alcohol.* My soul was screaming, "Pick me! Pick me!" I know that is not what this disease is about, but I am going there anyway with him. I wanted to fix him. Badly. I wanted to set him free. I want him that much. I know God put us together for a reason. To show us what His love is all about. Bob Goff says in his book, "I used to want to fix people, but now I just want to be with them" (2012, 1). Well, I was halfway there. I wanted to be with him one last time on this trip. I cringe when I think of my ulterior motives.

One of the things I learned about following Jesus is that He is full of surprises! Scott came with me on the trip … sober! This was the first seven days of our twenty-four years together spent in sobriety. The most precious, glorious, magnificent, delirious, dazzling days of my life with him. He even made his happy sounds when we were white-water rafting in West Virginia. I realized when I heard those sounds that I had not heard them in years. And I liked living from this place of pure delight. I felt like a small child, playing helplessly amidst the joyful sounds around me.

He flew home from Pennsylvania, and I continued the drive on to Massachusetts, alone. Well, Jesus was in the seat next to me, so never alone, alone. I participated in a yoga and recovery conference with one hundred souls gathered together with a collective intention of sharing sobriety and yoga. I had never been to a conference with one hundred people who at the bottom of their addiction found yoga. In the middle of all of them, I took on yoga with a sincere yearning to sit quietly and watch what would happen next. Well, something unexpected happened next all right.

Are you ready? Here's what happened. I was on a break from a yoga session, lying on the beach by a shimmering lake. We were supposed to be off grid, but I had my cell phone with me to check the time. (Of course, my phone was just with me so I wouldn't be late for the next session). It was on silent. I noticed a missed call from a private number. I must confess that I did a quick flashback to helicopter mom mode. I thought my son was in trouble again. Or there was an emergency at home. Old habits die hard. But I found myself sneaking off to the side of the boat house. I took a deep breath and listened to the message. Lo and behold, it was the secretary of the president of the university where I taught. She was calling to tell me the president needed to speak with me. Time for a little freak out. Thought I was in trouble. Like I was getting called to the principal's office at school. Nonetheless, I was able to overcome my fears and call the secretary back. She put me through to the president.

I was standing in the sand, on that beach, by the boathouse, by the lake as the president delivered the news that I won the Presidential Award for Excellence in Service for our university. Which would be accompanied by $5,000! Now that was quite a spot to be standing. A true witness to God's gift in sobriety. All that service I did to win that award, I did sober. My service consisted of using God's gifts of yoga and recreation therapy to love and care for persons with disabilities. That spot in the sand, on that beach, is where He confirmed that I am right where He wanted me to be. Just like in *Eat, Pray, Love* where Elizabeth recalls a Sufi poem. It goes something like … "A long time ago, God drew a circle in the sand around this exact spot where you are standing right now. This was never not going to happen. You were never not coming here" (Gilbert 2010, 80). That is exactly the spot where I stood. I called my husband and shared my tears of joy. Then I called my daddy. Cried some more. These big tears were the same size as my old jail tears. How far I have come. I like everything about the way this is turning out.

I spent another week at the yoga center being an assistant in chair yoga teacher training. During that time, God amazed me again when He introduced me to someone at the center who was new to navigating a sober life. We got to share so much support, love, and respect for each other's journeys. I told her of my upcoming fourth-year-of-sobriety birthday. It is not ironic to me that God told me to tell her about what He had done for me. After all, it is part of staying sober to carry the message to others. I also wanted to share my favorite yoga tips that I learned during those two weeks immersed in yoga. You can find them in appendix B.

Time to go home. I had always wanted to drive across the country by myself. Well, I did just that. I drove home singing to Jesus on the radio. On my first day, I saw a roadside cross. I had to pull over to take a picture of it. I drove across this dirt road in a field to get to it. As I pulled up, a man was there in his truck. He got out. He asked what I was doing. I replied, "I am a big fan of Jesus, and I wanted to say a prayer at this cross for a safe journey home." He told me that he was the pastor at that very church. He was retiring the next week. He asked to say a blessing over my journey home. Now that's what I am talking about! I roared a resounding, "Yes!" I took his picture by the cross.

I saw even more evidence of Jesus along the way home with other huge roadside crosses in Virginia and Tennessee. I stopped in Nashville and went to a church there because I missed worshipping with others. I missed being surrounded by believers. I craved singing and holding my hands up and dancing for Him. My husband thinks it is funny that I think Jesus likes it when I sing and dance for Him. Like God has nothing better to do than watch and listen to me when all these other Big things are going on in the world. Like when I make good rice (which I almost never can do), and I say, "That was Jesus blessing the rice!" I think Jesus delights in the small things, like perfectly made rice.

Next stop was Hot Springs, Arkansas, where I just happened upon a historic hotel that advertised a cupcake shop that had been on "Cupcake Wars" on the Cooking Channel! I had to go see it. Guess what T-shirt they had in their shop? It said "Yoga and Cupcakes." What? So I bought it. I am going to be on that show one day with my Jesus cupcakes to share His message: "Taste and see the goodness of the Lord."

When I finally arrived home, my husband gave me a gift bag in honor of my Presidential Award. It contained a one-of-a-kind string of mala beads he made from mountain laurel beans. He even added some rare yellow ones. He had drilled 108 beans! He attached charms with cupcakes and crosses. He got me a T-shirt that my stepdaughter found featuring a girl doing a yoga pose dreaming about cupcakes. I wore it for three days straight. He also got me concert tickets to see one of my favorite Christian artists, Danny Gokey! I expressed to him how blessed I was that in his gift he had honored my love of cupcakes, yoga, and Jesus. He was so surprised and unaware that he had done that. Awe ... Then he helped me come up with a list of Jesus tips. They are featured in appendix C.

I guess you are wondering how it is going since I have returned. I know I would be. Let's see ... He has climbed aboard the sober, white-water vacation raft with me and Jesus and has not gotten out. He is okay. He is healing. He is moving closer to me and God. We were in church together the other day and heard the sermon about Luke 8 22–25 when Jesus was in the boat with the disciples, in the storm, and they are scared, and He stayed in the boat with them, and asked, "Where is your faith?" Our vacation raft is that boat. We have faith in God that He will calm whatever storms come next. My husband told me I needed a new bumper sticker that says, "Love is staying in the boat." So I actually made two of them for our twenty-year anniversary. One for his truck this time too. He also showed me his latest garage fridge renovation. Instead of being full of beer, it is filled with various jugs of water. You go, Scott!

So for right now, we are placing our faith in Jesus and staying in the boat together. Even through the rapids ahead, we are just going to let Jesus be our river guide. With Scott making his happy sounds like on our white-water raft trip down the rapids in West Virginia. I asked Scott how he was doing being sober, and he said, "I am not drinking because it was getting in the way of our relationship." Miracle number twelve! I am not sure all the other miracles I will experience, but I know three things to be true ... that I love Jesus, yoga, and cupcakes.

All my joy,
Dr. Lyn

P. S. I was in my prayer warrior closet the other day and God spoke to me again... He said, "I am taking you somewhere, somewhere greater than you think." It was 11:11am.

All My Joy Cupcakes

(Makes 20 cupcakes)

Cupcake Ingredients:
1 3/4 cups unbleached all-purpose flour (sifted)
2 teaspoons baking powder
1/2 teaspoon salt
1/2 cup sweetened, shredded coconut
4 extra-large eggs (room temperature), divided
1 1/2 sticks unsalted butter (softened)
1 1/3 cups sugar
1 1/2 teaspoons vanilla extract
1 1/2 teaspoons almond extract
3/4 cup coconut milk

Ganache Frosting:
1 cup heavy whipping cream
8 ounces dark chocolate chips
1 tablespoon unsalted butter

Fluffy Dark Chocolate Filling:
1 (3-ounce) box instant dark chocolate pudding
1 1/2 cups heavy whipping cream
1/2 cup milk
1/4 cup sour cream

Garnish and Toppers:
1 1/2 cups flaked, toasted, sweetened coconut
20 toasted whole almonds
20 toothpicks with coconut decoration
20 "All My Joy" sayings

Directions:
- Preheat oven to 350 degrees F. Line cupcake tins with color-stay papers.
- Sift flour, baking powder, salt, and coconut in separate bowl.
- In electric mixer, whip 3 egg whites till soft peaks form. Scoop into separate bowl and set aside.
- In same mixer, whisk unsalted butter, sugar, and extracts till fluffy.
- Add 3 egg yolks, one at a time. Add last full egg.
- Alternate adding coconut milk and dry ingredients, and mix just till incorporated.
- Fold in egg whites, just till combined.
- Bake for 20 minutes or till toothpick comes out clean. Cool completely.

Ganache Frosting:
- Heat heavy whipping cream to a simmer.
- Place dark chocolate chips in a microwave-safe bowl.
- Pour heated cream over chocolate. Add butter and let stand for one minute. Mix completely.

Filling:
- In electric mixer, whip pudding, heavy whipping cream, milk, and sour cream till fluffy.
- Place in piping bag.
- Cut hole in center of cupcakes and fill with pudding mixture.
- Dip filled cupcakes into ganache, twirl, and lift.
- Place one almond in center of ganache-frosted cupcake.

Garnish and Topper:
- Spread flaked coconut on baking pan in oven at 350.
- Check frequently and stir till just browned. Cool completely.

Or you can buy pre-toasted coconut flakes.

- Use hand to gently pat coconut around edges of each cupcake.
- Cut out small sayings. Use glue gun to adhere to top of toothpick.

APPENDIX A

Lil Luna's Favorite Cupcake Tips

Learned from Make It Sweet Bakery, Austin, Texas (2016)

General Tips:
- Buy an electronic scale with a tare button; it will change your baking life.
- Did you know that liquids and fats weigh the same but dry ingredients vary in density? So use a scale to measure. For example: 1 cup sugar = 7 ounces; one large egg = 1.6 or 7 ounces; (egg white is 1 ounce, and yoke 6 ounces).
- When baking, all cold ingredients should be the same temperature. Room temperature is best.
- Use paddle attachment for mixing batters and frostings unless you are whipping cream or egg whites.
- Ever wonder about differences in flour? Pastry flour is the finest; followed by cake flour, which has a softer crumb; then all-purpose flour, which is sturdier; and finally bread flour, which is much denser and gets crusty.
- Use coarse kosher salt in recipes. It adds a flavor change on your tongue.
- Making simple syrup is simple. Combine one-part water with one-part sugar. Microwave for thirty seconds till sugar is dissolved.
- You can freeze egg whites but not the yokes.
- Have bananas that are too ripe to eat and want to save to bake with another day? Peel them and place in airtight container in freezer (one month) or (refrigerate one night).

- Having trouble separating eggs? If you drop some egg yolk into egg whites, use a piece of the egg shell and dip in egg whites; it should attract the yoke, and you can scoop it out.
- You can also separate egg whites from yolks by cracking whole egg in a bowl and using an empty squeeze bottle to suck up the yolks.
- If whipping egg whites and sugar for homemade marshmallow or angel food cupcakes, whisk on high until stiff, shiny peaks form and mixture pulls away from side of bowl. If you overmix, it will go back to liquid.
- If making angel food cupcakes, do not use papers or grease the cupcake tins; they won't rise.

Batter Tips:
- You can store cupcakes in airtight containers on countertop for one week; fridge for one month; or freeze for six months.
- You should sift all dry ingredients together and whisk so ingredients will be evenly distributed in batter.
- When combining batter ingredients, start with dry and end with liquid, one-third at a time; that way less gluten forms, and liquid brings it all together at the end.
- If using nuts in a batter, toast in oven first so they bake properly.
- Having cupcake dome troubles? Check your oven temperature; it could be off. Get an oven thermometer to verify exact temperature. Also check to see that your baking soda and powder are still fresh. Look at expiration dates or see if they fizz in water.

Frosting Tips:
- You can prepare most frostings in advance and store in airtight container in refrigerator for one week or freeze for up to six months. Then bring to room temperature and rewhip.
- Butter melts faster than shortening in frostings, so if you live in the South, beware. Also best shortening to use is called Higher Ratio Shortening. It has a better taste.
- Use icing fruits or zest instead of fresh fruit in frostings, as they will hold the color better, and frosting will hold its integrity.

Substitutions or DIY:

- You can substitute sour cream in a recipe with yogurt or mashed bananas. Just substitute by weight.
- Out of brown sugar? Just add 1 tablespoon molasses to white sugar and mix.
- You can substitute eggs with apple sauce or tofu. Just go by weight to make substitutions.
- Make your own buttermilk by adding 1–2 tablespoons of vinegar or lemon juice to 1 cup of milk and stir.
- Need baking powder? Just mix 1 tablespoon baking soda with 2 tablespoons cream of tartar. Voila!

APPENDIX B

Yoga Tips

Learned from: Lakshmi Voelker Chair Yoga Teacher Training (2016); Soma Institute: Integrative Yoga Therapy (2015); Yoga, Meditation, and Recovery Conference (Gates, et al. 2016).

Favorite tip: *Yoga is a process of becoming your own best friend.* (Needs to be a bumper sticker.)

Need to reduce your stress levels? Try yoga practice. It takes you out of "flight, fight, or freeze" mode into rest and digest restoration mode.

Need to lose weight and get healthy? Try Senobi breath before each meal. Before each meal, sit or stand in a firm mountain pose. Raise arms above your head (palms flat facing ceiling with fingers pointing back). Gaze where the ceiling and wall meet, arching the back, slightly drawing shoulder blades down and together. Then breathe in your nostrils to the count of five and exhale through your nostrils to the count of five. Repeat three times. Then interlace your fingers with arms still raised above the head and repeat breath cycle three times.

Have a craving you want to avoid? Shut your right nostril and breathe in and out of the left one for three minutes.

Low on energy or feeling sluggish? Shut your left nostril and breathe in and out of the left one for three minutes.

Want to feel high without drugs or alcohol? Do the "happy hour" pose (aka, legs up the wall or waterfall). It will give you the same high as that first sip, but it's chemical-free! Lay on your back and scoot your bum up against a wall. Straighten your legs to rest on the wall. Or you can use a chair and rest your legs from the knee down on the seat of the chair. Do for five to fifteen minutes a day. Cheers!

Having trouble staying focused in the now? Worrying about past or future? Focus on your breath. You can't breathe in the past or the future, only the now.

Having trouble quieting your mind? Great analogy for you to ponder: Silence in yoga holds all the noise, just like the sky holds all the weather.

Having difficulty with meditation? Think you can't focus or eliminate distractions? Just inhale and exhale to:

"So Hum" (I am that; I am that I am). Inhale in your nose to "So" and exhale through your mouth "Hum." Try it for six minutes a day for six months and see how you feel. More peace? Joy? Tranquility? Less stress, anxiety, and depression?

Need to detoxify your liver or reduce your anger? Do the essential movement called "clenching fists with attentive eyes." Punch one arm/fist at a time to the front of your body—to the right and left sides, then to the ceiling, then to the floor—all while saying aloud "Ha" as you exhale out of your mouth. Repeat three times.

Experienced a trauma? Addiction is undigested trauma. Focus on grounding poses (e.g., standing; or supine/prone; or balance) and holding them for three to five breaths, versus doing flowing poses of one breath per movement. Provides more support, safety, and predictability. Use props for support and security.

Are you addicted to busy? Not enoughness? Too muchness? Check out Patanalis Yoga Sutra's Yamas and Niyamas. They remind me of the Ten Commandments. Live your yoga life off the mat.

Get a crick in your neck? Shoulder tension or back ache? Take care of your body parts that need extra healing in the office or while on computer. Roll your feet on top of a tennis ball. All over the bottom of the toes, arch, outside of foot and heel. Foot reflexology can really change the way you take care of you.

Did you know sighing is good for you? Do it more often, and it will bring you relief and improves lungs.

Experiencing a digestive problem? IBS? Constipation? Nourish your body mind and soul and relieve dis-ease. Check out your Dosha type using Ayurveda nutritional system. It is a wonderful partner to yoga practice. I lost fifteen pounds in a year, and my IBS symptoms are relieved.

Having trouble finding your passion or your voice? Doing backbends or inversions opens your heart and throat chakras. Get ready—it is going to happen!

Are you great at self-criticism or comparing yourself to others during yoga? Visualize your yoga mat or chair as a judgment-free zone. Accept who and what you are in that space. That way you can bypass your ego.

Having difficulty going to sleep? Practice Yoga Nidra. It will create a quiet space in your mind and take you to the state of your tipping point right before you drop into sleep.

Are you stuck in athlete mentality of "no pain, no gain"? Choose "no pain, no pain." Yoga shouldn't hurt. Honor your body. Use props that will support your practice.

Holding on to pent-up emotions? Try hip opener to release them. Be prepared, as they may come out when you least expect it. Here is my favorite way to do a hip opener. Take a chair without arms and flip it over on the floor so that the outside back of the chair faces up and a gentle slope is formed. Lay a blanket over the sloped back of chair. Sit on the floor in front of the sloped back padded chair and lean back to lay on the slope. Your hips will be bent at about a 45-degree angle. Bend your legs at the knees, put your feet together towards the center line of your body, about 1ft or so in front of your hips on the floor. Drop your knees out wide to each side of your body (away from center... to right and left). Using two yoga blocks or pillows tuck them for support under the outside of both of your knees. Lay back and just breath naturally for 1-5 minutes.

Having difficulty being versus doing yoga? Look at yoga through the lens of the koshas. You will learn not to just *do* a pose but to *be* a pose. You will also find your true essence of your being. Start with trying on a yoga pose like you try on clothes. See how they fit and feel on and in your body.

Afraid to go upside down? Try doing a shoulder stand between two padded chairs up against a wall. Place chairs sideways so the seats face each other about head-width apart. Make sure chairs are secure up against the wall. Kneel down in front of opening between chairs and place your head between the opening. Begin to straighten your legs and place your shoulders on seat cushions till you feel secure and supported. (You may need to adjust the closeness of the chairs to fit your shoulders). Then grab onto seat of chairs that are facing away from the wall with both hands (one on each chair). Hitch your legs up above your head so they are supported by the wall. Stay as long as you like (one to five minutes is fine). As you gain more stability and control, try holding your legs up without using the wall. Keep the chairs by the wall for rest. First time you try it, get someone to spot you for safety. It will change the way you see a problem. Give you a new perspective on a situation. Improves digestion and heart function.

APPENDIX C

Jesus Tips

Gathered from various sources by Lyn and Scott Litchke

- If God can work through me, he can work through anyone.
- God is bigger than people think.
- Life is God's novel; let Him write it.
- God never ends anything on a negative—always a positive.
- What God intended for you goes far beyond anything you can imagine.
- If you have resentment against God, you believe in God.
- You have to fight to stay naive. Give God a second chance.
- God is offering more. He is patient and will wait and offer again and again. It is never too late.
- Jesus will love you until you learn to love Him back. Start by loving yourself and others.
- Jesus did not come for the perfect people. He came for you and me. Don't disqualify yourself.
- God does not call the ones He equips. He equips the ones He calls. Answer the phone, text, or tweet …
- Are you done answering the questions God did not ask?
- God can't drive a parked car.
- Getting saved is like going from living in black-and-white to living color!
- Having no plan is a plan. God has a plan for you. It's gonna be wild. It's gonna be great. It's gonna be full of Him.
- Every day become the best version of yourself. Do one holy moment at a time. God is not in the business of *tweaking*. He is the business of *transforming* (Kelly 2015).

- Praying is talking to God. Mediating is listening to Him.
- Pray big and don't get attached to the results. Leave the results up to God. He will surprise you beyond your wildest expectation. Get ready to be amazed!
- What is greater, your fear or your faith? Are you afraid to be free?
- There are two sides to every chain. What's on the other end of your chain?
- Forgiveness is contagious! Forgive someone. Forgive yourself. Ask, accept, and live forgiven.
- Text someone: URFREE24GIVE.
- Through every storm, Jesus is in the boat. You need to get in the boat. Love is staying in the boat even in troubled waters.
- Lay success and failure at God's feet.
- Can you trust God? Even if you do not understand His ways? Even if it's dark and you cannot see where He is taking you? Even if there is no reassurance? Even if you do not feel His presence? (D'Arcy 1996).
- Can you see God without your eyes? Try using your third eye … your spiritual eye of yoga.
- It is hard to find God when only darkness is showing. I found God in yoga. Yoga shows you the light. God is your flashlight. He will illuminate your path.
- God is in the thin places. Where is your thin place? Wherever you feel awe inspired, that is your thin place.
- Warning! Better isn't always easier.
- Jesus miracle: Changing water to wine. Bigger miracle: Changing wine back to water! I did. You can too.
- Guru means: GU=darkness, RU=light. God is my guru! Out of the darkness into the light.

ACKNOWLEDGMENTS

I could not have written these words unless God had surrounded me with such loving family, friends, AA, inspirational books and music, and Christian counselors. First and foremost, to my husband, Scott, I know that God put us together for a reason … to get in the boat with Him. You show me everything I need to see about myself. It is your turn to be happy, baby. Thanks for turning your booze back to water.

To my two sons, if there were one thousand boys lined up in a row, I would pick you two to be mine. To my oldest son, Nic, I treasure our shared passion for animated Pixar and Disney films but mostly the way you live your life without judgment of yourself and others. You truly live a life full of joy! What a huge gift you are to this world, your family, and your mom.

To my baby son, Zac, I can see the beauty of your spirit every time I look at you or hear your voice. It took so much courage for you to join me on this writing adventure. You are the reason I found Jesus, sobriety, yoga, and myself. Tag, you're it … My love goes out to Chelsea Rae, thank you, sweet gal, for showing Zac and I your passion for us and yoga!

To my stepchildren, Jared and Sammy, thank you so much for always treating me with such kindness and inspiring me with your quirky senses of humor. You have always been so special to me. To my daddy and sweet sisters, you have known me longer than anyone on this earth, and you each own a piece of my heart. When we are together, I find myself craving a car picnic.

This book and my life would not be the same without all my dearest friends. Matt and Trish, you are the closest two people to family I have ever known. I was never more certain than the day Matt came to my son's rescue. And the day, Trish, you called me to watch your children when you needed help. Those two events were turning points in my recovery. Thank you for loving me and Scott through it all for over twenty years. To Molly and Jason, what a gift you bestowed on me to help you with your twins. Another reward of my sobriety and our friendship. Jo Jo, my adventurous friend who walked, ran, swam, and rode so much of this path with me. May you always know how much you are loved. Anna, those cards you sent my son in jail gave us the strength to get through those one hundred days. I am forever grateful. Stephanie W., thank you for giving me my first Bible and God's most comforting angels. Mari and Brenda, who remain such loyal and supportive friends, we are truly lifetime RIOSA sisters. To my Ridge gals, Liz, Leti, and Brooke, thank you for your lifetime of friendship and all we have persevered through together.

To Marcus M. and all the residents at Sodalis Elder Living, I learned more from you than you can ever imagine. Thanks for sharing your lives and yoga with me. To the most beautiful family at Texas Ski Ranch, the Bialicks, you helped save Zac and my life. I am forever blessed by knowing you. Thank you for opening your business and hearts to help all people heal. Mr. Hendry, Allie, Jes, Jan, and Lisa, you are my rocks of support at the university. You are such great examples of the power of a loving working family.

To my dearest high school best friend, Susie, you have gone out of your way to reach out and stay connected with me over the past thirty years. My life would not be the same without you. Ellen and Mark, thank you for allowing me to be honest with you and share my journey in sobriety.

To all my recreation therapy students who supported me in my walk with Jesus. Heather, thank you for getting all my Lynisms and reconnecting with me along this journey called life. Audrey, Daniel, Ducky, Meagan, Rachel, Katie, Michaela, Michelle, Brad, Bethany, Chase, Christina, and Stephanie D., keep shining your lights on everyone through recreation. To my CRU friends, Craig and Ginger Corley, thank you for giving me the courage and opportunity to share my story with other college students.

A big bouquet for my two Christian counselors, Kelly Zentner from Stepping Forward Christian Counseling in Garden Ridge, Texas, and Richard Laosa from Guadalupe Valley Christian Counseling Center in Seguin, Texas, you are part of God's saving army of angels on this earth. You shine light into dark places. Thank you for illuminating my path to Jesus.

I bow in gratitude to my lovely yoga teacher Lakshmi Voelker and her husband, Bruce Binder, learning chair yoga from Get Fit Where You Sit teacher training (2010–2016) launched me on my spiritual journey to freedom and God. Thank you for guiding me home. Liz and Molly, from Soma Yoga Institute (2015) in Hawaii, you gave me the most beautiful eyes to see the true essence in myself that I needed to come home and begin writing this book.

Thank you to my AA sponsor, Karen. Without you, I would not have "worked" my steps. Mama D, wherever life takes you, keep on sharing your Big Island AA love. Thanks for celebrating my third year of sobriety with me. Mahalo.

Finally, I would like to give a standing ovation to authors, speakers, Bob Goff (2012), Kevin Breel (2015), Mathew Kelly (2015), and Christian music artist Danny Gokey. Your presentations, books, and music taught me to undue my shame, share my story, launch numerous Operation Love Does missions for Jesus, and write in my Mass journal each Sunday. Just busy tweaking and transforming. I am all yours, God. How can I help?

Danny, will you sing the soundtrack for the movie about this book?

ABOUT THE AUTHOR

Dr. Lyn Gorbett Litchke is an associate professor of recreation therapy at Texas State University in San Marcos, where she has taught since 2002. She is the 2016 recipient of the Presidential Award for Excellence in Service. She has been a certified therapeutic recreation specialist for over twenty-five years. Lyn has practiced in early intervention, physical rehabilitation, and psychiatric hospitals for twenty years prior to getting her doctorate in adult professional and community education at Texas State and teaching there. She is a certified Lakshmi Voelker chair yoga teacher and two-hundred-hour integrative yoga therapist. Her yoga and meditation research is dedicated to helping persons with Alzheimer's disease and those who love and care for them; youth with autism spectrum disorder; and Wounded Warriors on the water engaging in paddleboard yoga.

Her son Zac completed his chair yoga certification with Lakshmi and just finished his two-hundred-hour yoga teacher training course. Zac and his mom continue to bring the healing magic of yoga to persons who need it most.

Dr. Lyn, as she is called by her students, is still pursuing God and all His wonder for her life. She is sober and symptom-free of IBS and anxiety, thanks to cupcakes, yoga, and Jesus! By the way, this is being published in honor of her fourth sober birthday! Best birthday ever!

BIBLIOGRAPHY

Arterburn, Stephen and Stoop, David. *Life Recovery Bible New Living Translation*. Second edition. Carol Stream: Tyndale House Publishers, Inc., 1998.

Bachman, Nicolai. *The Path of the Yoga Sutras: A Practical Guide to the Core of Yoga*. Boulder: Sounds True, Inc., 2011.

Benton, Sarah A. *Understanding the High-Functioning Alcoholic: Breaking the Cycle and Finding Hope*. Lanham: Rowen and Littlefield, 2010.

Breel, Kevin. *Boy Meets Depression: Or Life Sucks and Then You Live*. New York: Harmony Books, 2015.

Carr, Allen. *The Easy Way to Stop Drinking*. New York City: Sterling, 2005.

D'Arcy, Paula. *Gift of the Red Bird: A Spiritual Encounter*. New York: Crossroad Publishing Company, 1996.

Gates, Rolf, Nikki Myers, Tommy Rosen, Melody Moore, Tim Walsh, and Aruni Nan Futuronsky. *Yoga, Meditation, and Recovery Conference*. Kripalu, Massachusetts. May 30–June 3, 2016.

Gilbert, Elizabeth. *Eat, Pray, Love: One Woman's Search for Everything Across Italy, India and Indonesia*. New York: Penguin Books, 2010.

Goff, Bob. *Love Does: Discover A Secretly Incredible Life in an Ordinary World*. Nashville: Thomas Nelson, 2012.

Gorbett, Ann. Blog. *Palette Knife Paintings*. http://anngorbett.blogspot.com/.

Kelly, Mathew. *Rediscover Jesus: An Invitation*. Rochester: Publishing, 2015.

Le Page, Joseph. *Integrative Yoga Therapy: Yoga Teacher Training Manual*. 2007.

Litchke, Lyn G. and Jan S. Hodges. "The Meaning of 'Now' Moments of Engagement in Yoga for Persons with Alzheimer's Disease." *Therapeutic Recreation Journal* 48, no. 3 (2014): 229–246.

Litchke, Lyn. G., Jan S. Hodges, and Robert F. Reardon. "Benefits of Adaptive Yoga for Persons with Mild to Severe Alzheimer's Disease." *Activities, Adaptations and Aging* 36, no. 4 (2012): 317–328.

Make It Sweet. *All in One Bake Shop*. Accessed May 10, 2016. https://www.allinonebakeshop.com/documents/AIOBScupcakeflavors.pdf

New King James Version (NKJV). *The Holy Bible*. Nashville: Thomas Nelson Publishers, 1982.

Santas, Dana. *Beyond Namaste: The Benefits of Yoga in Schools.* Accessed on May 10, 2016. http://www.cnn.com/2016/05/10/health/yoga-in-schools/.

Smith, Bob and Wilson, Bill. *Big Book of Alcoholics Anonymous.* New York City: Alcoholics Anonymous World Services, Inc., 2001.

Soma Yoga Institute. *200-Hour Therapeutic Yoga Teacher Training.* Kalani, Hawaii. July 7–31, 2015.

Tack, Karen and Richardson, Alan. *cupcakes, cookies, & pies, oh, my!* New York: Houghton Mifflin Harcourt Company, 2012.

Television Food Network. "Cupcake Wars." Accessed May 18, 2016. http://www.foodnetwork.com/shows/cupcake-wars.html/.

Voelker, Lakshmi. *Get Fit Where You Sit Chair Yoga Teacher Training.* Kripalu, Massachusetts. June 5–10, 2016.

War Room: Prayer is a Powerful Weapon, directed by Alex Kendrick. 2015. Culver City, CA: Sony Pictures, 2015. DVD.

Watts, Alan. W. Quotes. Accessed on May 1, 2016. http://www.goodreads.com/quotes/227233-look-here-is-a-tree-in-the-garden-and-every.

Young, William P. *The Shack: Where Tragedy Confronts Eternity.* Newbury Park: Windblown Media, 2007.

Printed in the United States
By Bookmasters